KENT
PORTS AND
HARBOURS

While most of this book deals with the ships and the seafarers who have sailed and still sail from the Kent ports, it is important to remember that for around 200 years a number of them have been very popular seaside resorts where people manage to forget their cares for a weekend or a week or two. Such people want a reminder of their time spent by the sea and beach photographers satisfied that need. A stuffed lion served as a prop for a long time on the promenade at Cliftonville, and this picture captures an element of our youth and the more placid times of half a century ago. (Sunbeam Photos)

KENT
PORTS AND
HARBOURS

ANTHONY LANE

To Captain Alan Jenner of the motor barge Roffen; *Michael Hunt, until recently Curator of Ramsgate Maritime Museum and Captain John Megoran of the* Kingswear Castle, *who have given in turn many years of service to Crescent Shipping, much enlightenment of the port's history to Ramsgate's visitors, and many a day's enjoyable steaming aboard the last coal-burning British paddle steamer.*

First published 2010

The History Press
The Mill, Brimscombe Port
Stroud, Gloucestershire, GL5 2QG
www.thehistorypress.co.uk

British Library Cataloguing in Publication Data.
A catalogue record for this book is available from the British Library.

ISBN 978 0 7524 5363 7

Typesetting and origination by The History Press
Printed in Great Britain

CONTENTS

Acknowledgements

M any people have helped me with information relating to the ports and harbours of Kent. I would particularly like to thank Michael Hunt and Bob Bradley of the Ramsgate Maritime Museum and the Margate Local History Museum, without whose help it would have been difficult to complete those two chapters. Additionally, Mike Gambrill at Whitstable Harbour helped to provide many interesting details on the earlier operation of the harbour.

Amongst the various representatives of the harbour authorities I would like to record my sincere thanks to Kevin Beacon, assistant harbourmaster at Sheerness, and his pilot colleagues for taking the time to explain in detail the many facets of Medway Ports and for providing contacts to agents and staff at other berths on that river. In returning to the Sheerness VTS, I was able to revive old friendships with those I got to know during the preparation of *Maritime Kent*. They were kind enough to acquaint me with the many changes that have occurred since the writing of that book some ten years ago.

I would also like to thank both staff at the Port of Dover and representatives of the ferry companies Norfolk Line, Seafrance and LD Ferries, who explained their new ships to me in detail. I mention particularly Commandant Ludovic Delarouzee of *Seafrance Berlioz* and Captain Mike Andrew of *Maersk Delft*.

A number of people have kindly allowed their photographs to be included in the historical part of this work, including Geoff Michell, Ron Kite, Ray Harrison and Duncan Francis. It has equally been of great interest to learn of the history and current operations of the ports from people of such varied background.

INTRODUCTION

The County of Kent has a long coastline with one major river, the Medway, some minor ones of which the principal is the Stour, and many various creeks. It also forms for some distance the southern bank of the Thames. Over the centuries many different harbours and piers have been built, initially for the use of fishermen but later also for small ships carrying produce to London and other ports around the coast. To list all of these ports is difficult, as some tended to rise into prominence according to the demand for a certain product or service and then fade away when it was no longer needed or vessels became too large to be accommodated.

A number of Kent's ports have a long history. In historical records they first come to prominence in Roman times, when Richborough (Rutupiae), Reculver (Regulbium), Dover (Dubris) and Lympne (Portus Lemanis) all played an important part in sustaining the occupying forces; Richborough becoming the main port of supply for the Roman Legions in Britain. Dover is the only Roman port active today but it also has the further significance of being the base for the Classis Britannica, or Roman Fleet, in British waters. Considering its closeness to Europe, it is not surprising that Dover remained important after the Romans had departed.

The League of the Cinque Ports was established around the eleventh century, and thus Hastings, Dover, Romney, Hythe and Sandwich became providers of a fleet for the defence of the nation, the forerunner of the Royal Navy. Their period of importance extended almost to the time of the Spanish Armada in 1588, but by then the continual drift of sand and shingle due to the eastward tidal stream of the English Channel had largely closed all but Dover, which managed to survive in spite of the invading shingle, and retained its importance as the major port for Channel crossings, a position which was reinforced by the arrival of the railway. Folkestone also benefited in the same way, but it was Dover that attracted the most traffic, whether pilgrims, motorists, or more recently, coaches and freight vehicles.

It was during the Tudor period that Chatham became a naval dockyard, and for some time was the most important in the land. Sheerness followed in the same capacity in the time of Charles II. Warships were built in considerable numbers at Chatham up until 1967, and at Sheerness until 1903. Kent saw great military activity during the First and Second World Wars, with both naval yards working to full capacity. In the earlier conflict, Richborough became the 'Mystery Port' which built barges and supplied the Western Front. Dover at that time achieved fame for the tenacity and achievements of the Dover Patrol. Although the Navy withdrew after the cessation of hostilities, warships returned to Dover on a small scale during the second period of conflict, using it as a base for destroyers until the port was made untenable by German air attacks. Later it housed minesweepers. In May 1940, the harbour provided a relatively safe haven from which to organise the evacuation of Dunkirk and a place capable of accepting an enormous number of evacuees.

The second half of the twentieth century saw the cessation of all naval activities in the county, and the ports concerned were left to develop their facilities as much as possible, which Sheerness and Chatham did successfully in their different ways. The last sixty years have in fact seen great commercial growth in the major ports of Dover, Sheerness and Ramsgate. The Chatham Dockyard complex has become part museum, part marina, part commercial port and part housing development. No commercial vessels now call at Faversham or Sandwich, but the former still has boatyards and caters particularly for the needs of leisure sailors and sailing barges. Folkestone and Ramsgate still have fishing, but by way of contrast, the latter has become a cross-Channel ferry port, maintaining a regular Ostend service, while at Folkestone the service has ceased. In contrast, Dover has seen the size of the Channel ferries and frequency of services increase so much that it now claims to be the busiest ferry port in the world.

As so many Kent ports have existed at one time or another, a choice has to be made over which to include in a work of this dimension. The Thames-side piers and wharves are excluded as they will be covered in a separate work devoted to that river. Included are the major harbours of the Medway, because of their long history and continuing importance. Margate and Ramsgate are described in detail because they drew considerable wealth from passenger traffic by sea, becoming resorts famous for sea-bathing. Margate, sadly, is little used as a harbour nowadays, and with the exception of that town and Folkestone, ports have been chosen which are still commercially active.

The Cinque Ports

As the south-east coast was frequently subjected to attacks by invaders, the defence of the seaboard of the realm became gradually more organised. The ultimate result was the formation of the Confederation of the 'five' or Cinque Ports, probably around the time of Edward the Confessor. While Dover, Sandwich, Hythe, Romney and Hastings became the head ports, all of the lesser Kentish harbours were gradually drawn in as limbs to support the King's requirements for ships when the country was threatened. Rye and Winchelsea were also incorporated, but as 'antient towns' rather than ports in their own right.

The Portsmen were given considerable privileges by the King, most importantly perhaps freedom from tax and tolls, which set them apart from other port dwellers, and these benefits were jealously guarded. In return for these privileges they were required to provide a fleet of fifty-seven ships for the defence of the realm for a period of fifteen days each year. Although there seems to have been variations in the number of ships provided by each port, the agreement was honoured until the fifteenth century, by which time the silting of Sandwich, Hythe and Romney led to their decline. As a consequence, Deal and Walmer, both non-corporate members of the Confederation, increased in strategic significance as they guarded the important naval anchorage of the Downs.

The modern Navy, which replaced the Cinque Ports Confederation, mainly owes its existence to Henry VII and Henry VIII, and it is from this Tudor period that we see the development of the large naval depots at Chatham and Sheerness.

Chatham and Rochester

Chatham essentially rose to prominence as a naval yard. A very large vessel for its time, the 600-ton, 100-gun *Grace Dieu* was built there as early as 1488. She was a very interesting ship because previously the majority of the fleet comprised merchant vessels converted in wartime to fighting ships, as used by the Cinque Ports. By 1547 there was a naval anchorage at 'Jillingham Water', and the Crown was renting storehouses ashore. A castle was built at Upnor in 1559–567 in order to provide protection for the naval yard, which soon became the most important in the kingdom, being given the title 'Chatham Dockyard' in 1567. The first ship to be officially launched from the yard was a 5-gun pinnace, the *Sunne*, in 1586. Shipbuilding became a major activity and some 500 ships were built there for the Navy during the next 400 years. Phineas Pett was appointed as Master Shipwright in 1605 and he and his family were influential in expanding the dockyard to include dry docks and rope-making facilities.

The growth of the yard and its apparent security under the guns of Upnor Castle was given a severe shock when the Dutch invaded the Medway in 1667. They first looted Sheerness and then broke through the chain barrier to reach Chatham. Upnor Castle proved ineffective, for the Dutch succeeded in burning ships assembled in the river. They also captured the flagship *Royal Charles*, which had brought Charles II back to the throne, sailing it to Holland.

HMS *Victory* remains the most famous ship built at Chatham. Her keel was laid in 1759 and she was completed in 1765. Other notable vessels were the *Achilles* of 1863, the first iron warship to be built in a royal dockyard, the battleship *Magnificent* of 14,900 tons launched in 1894, and following her, HMS *Africa* of 1905, at 16,350 tons the largest and also the last battleship built at the yard. The cruiser *Vindictive*, used for the Zeebrugge raid of St George's Day 1918, was also a Chatham product. After the Second World War construction was concentrated on submarines and the last ship built was the Canadian submarine *Okanagan* in 1967. Subsequently the dockyard became an important refitting base for nuclear submarines. However, the shallow approach waters of the Thames Estuary were eventually considered to leave them vulnerable to attack, and the depot ultimately closed.

There have been 'Navy Days' since 1928, which allowed the public to view the activities of the dockyard and watch special displays. These were held during most peacetime years, but the final ones planned for May 1982 were cancelled due to the Falklands War. A little earlier a defence assessment had decided that a base at Chatham was no longer necessary and, consequent to this, the Admiral's flag was hauled down on 30 September 1983 and the Navy left the site totally on 31 March 1984.

Since that date the oldest part of the site has been developed as a museum with a large number of interesting exhibits including the rope works and a separate RNLI museum. HMS *Ocelot*, a Chatham-built submarine, was returned after completion of her naval service and is preserved in a dry dock alongside the sloop HMS *Gannet* and the destroyer HMS *Cavalier*.

Rochester developed separately as a series of riverside wharves. Historically, lime kilns were built near to the riverbank which were fed by chalk quarried locally, giving their name to Limehouse Reach. Out of these early works a large cement industry developed that extended upriver towards Maidstone. More recently that trade has been replaced by the import of forest products in Scandinavian ships.

Acorn Shipyard close to Rochester Bridge was the base for the New Medway Steam Packet Co., whose passenger steamers carried the public down to the coast resorts of Margate and Ramsgate and across the estuary to Southend. The London & Rochester Trading Co. (later Crescent Shipping) also had a yard on the opposite bank which built barges for their coastal fleet. This area is now occupied by Denton Ship Repairers. Most of the Rochester town berths have since closed. Doust's Shipyard has long gone. Cory's, Stanley's and the Limehouse wharves have all been cleared, covered with spoil from the recent dredging of the Prince's Channel. Only a crane stands as a memorial to their earlier existence. Until recently the river below Rochester Bridge was a very busy one. Lapthorns, based further downriver at Buttercrock Wharf, Hoo, were successful in coastal shipping until recently, but they too have now ceased to operate.

Crown Wharf, the Scotline Berth and the Euro Aggregate Wharf opposite Chatham Dockyard still remain open, the first two handling forest products. Nowadays about the only vessels to have Rochester as their port of registry are four of Svitzer's tugs at Sheerness.

Sheerness

As Chatham gained in importance the entrance to the Medway also increased in significance. Early in the 1660s, King Charles II asked Samuel Pepys to examine the possibility of cleaning and refitting vessels at Sheerness rather than requiring them to go the further ten miles to Chatham. The works were still at an early stage when the Dutch arrived for their famous assault, breaking the sea defence walls and burning the port. Progress was still slow after that, but by 1668 the base began to take shape and provide a better defence against further attacks by the Dutch. During its construction the damp air and marshy land caused a lot of illness among the builders and fitters who were forced to live in converted wooden hulks. In spite of this, shipbuilding began by 1689 and the base became substantial enough to refit and repair the Nore Fleet during the Napoleonic Wars.

In 1813 John Rennie was asked to design and build an entirely new dockyard. The resulting construction, completed by 1826, consisted of a Great Basin with an entrance width of 63 ft, three dry docks and a wide range of administrative buildings with an outermost defence battery situated at Garrison Point. All of these were built on a region of soft mud and sand, a considerable achievement, most of the labour being supplied by French prisoners and English convicts. One ship of interest built at Sheerness is the sloop HMS *Gannet*, from the steam and sail era, which is presently preserved at Chatham. The largest ship built there was the cruiser HMS *Charybdis*, of 4,360 tons displacement, launched in 1893. Although shipbuilding largely ceased after 1903, Sheerness remained an important port for repair and refitting through the two world wars. Like Chatham, it suffered considerably from attacks by enemy aircraft. Then it sustained damage of a different kind in the floods of 1 February 1953, when the corvette *Berkeley Castle* capsized in a dry dock.

Change was also fast approaching, for the Navy gave up the yard altogether seven years later, ending 300 years of association with the Navy. In 1960 Sheerness became a 'Trust' Port, which was later sold to the management. A buyout by Mersey Docks and the Harbour Board followed, and currently the port is owned by Peel Ports, who own Mersey Docks, Manchester Ship Canal and numerous other undertakings. Sheerness is very different to Chatham nowadays, for while at the latter the site has been promoted as a museum with parts being sold for development, retaining only No. 3 basin as a dock for shipping, the former has exploited as far as possible its commercial potential. The remaining commercial Chatham Dock trades with Sheerness under the title Medway Ports.

The berths at the mouth of the Medway and on the Isle of Grain opposite have taken the lion's share of growth in cargo volume. The BP oil refinery was the first major installation to be opened at Grain in 1954, and its closure in 1984 was a severe blow. However, it was replaced fairly rapidly by the Thamesport container terminal, an aggregate berth receiving road-making material from Glensanda, and more recently by a BP liquid natural gas berth capable of accommodating tankers of more than 100,000 tons. A second jetty for this terminal is under construction. The power stations at Kingsnorth and Grain also have jetties on this side of the river. Coal is discharged at the former and oil at the more remote Oakham Ness, for the use of both stations, as required.

Ferries have operated on various occasions from the Medway. At the beginning of the twentieth century they ran from Queenborough to Flushing. At Sheerness, the Olau Line again ran ferries to

Flushing from 1974, eventually introducing the very large and comfortable 33,000-ton ferries *Olau Britannica* and *Olau Hollandia*. While this service ultimately ceased in 1994, fruit imports, timber and forest products remained strong. Sheerness has also become a major terminal for car imports, a large area of the Lappel Bank being reclaimed for their storage.

Medway Ports have overall responsibility for the maintenance of channels and reaches of the River Medway as far upstream as Allington Lock, a distance of twenty-three miles, and provide pilots for all commercial vessels over fifty metres in length berthing in the river or in Chatham Dock, Ridham Dock or Grovehurst Jetty.

Whitstable

Whitstable is a small municipal port famous for its oyster fishery dating back to Roman times. Nowadays there are about fourteen vessels fishing from the port, but only one vessel, the *Misty*, dredges all year round for oysters. One of the earlier yawls, the *Favourite*, F69, built in 1890, is preserved ashore as a tribute to this famous industry. The *Gamecock* (F76) of 1907 has also been restored and is sailed regularly by Bill Coleman.

Apart from fishing, this harbour enjoyed relatively little other maritime prosperity until the arrival of the railway in May 1830 when the Canterbury & Whitstable Railway Company introduced the world's first passenger and freight service on the 'Crab & Winkle Line' from Canterbury to the coast. The harbour was opened in 1832 and was mainly used by sailing colliers arriving from the Northumberland coalfield. Their cargoes were carried by railway to Canterbury and then distributed to the larger ports of Kent, some being carried further still as other lines developed. In the later Victorian period the Whitstable Shipping Co. owned a fleet of sailing ships of 150-250 tons, bringing coal to the harbour. Some of this coal was converted to coke for the use of the steam locomotives on the line by ovens situated on the harbour. These were demolished in 1892.

In parallel with the coal trade, other vessels were engaged in salvage work and the dispersion of wrecks. Alfred Gann & Co., established in 1873, worked on many wrecks around the south and east coasts and occasionally in Ireland, France and the low countries, some of which provided very considerable financial rewards. This activity became of such importance that a fraternity of divers was based in the town. The Whitstable Salvage Co. was formed in 1898 and this and others that followed employed divers to work at demolishing wrecks from the First and Second World Wars with explosive charges.

Experiments with the tarring of roads began in Kent in the early years of the twentieth century. The use of this material grew rapidly and the Kent Tarmacadam Co., later owned by Robert Brett & Sons, eventually built a plant on the East Quay of Whitstable Harbour in 1935–36 which could produce 40 tons of tarmac each hour. Bretts have remained at the harbour since that date, expanding their activities. Over the years they have received cargoes of limestone and granite chips as well as sand, sea-dredged aggregates and blast furnace slag. Crescent Shipping brought in a number of these cargoes, and then later, in the 1980s and 1990s, Lapthorn's *Hoo* ships called many times. Stone from Scotland and Granville in France is now delivered by the Union Transport Group, with whom Bretts have a contract, in vessels such as *Union Pluto* and *Union Neptune*, which call from fifty to sixty times a year.

Whitstable relies nowadays on three activities; fishing, the import of stone and the provision of facilities for the maintenance of the thirty turbines of the Kentish Flats wind farm.

Margate

Margate became a limb of the Cinque Port of Dover in 1229. At this time it had 108 inhabited houses and fifteen fishing boats. Its first harbour dates from 1320, from where sailing vessels carried barley, vegetables and fish to London. Thanet was well known for the yield and quality of barley that grew there, and those who worked on the land in the winter often turned to fishing in the summer months. The harbour, described by one as 'sore decayed' and later by Defoe, in 1701, as 'a poor pitiful place', was sufficient enough to be used occasionally as a point of departure and arrival for royalty. However, the fortunes of Margate were about to change.

In 1736 Thomas Barber advertised a salt water bath in the basement of his New Inn, and it was also at Margate that Benjamin Beale invented, in 1753, the first bathing machine with a modesty hood, which allowed bathers, particularly ladies, to undress and bathe in privacy. The hoys carrying local produce to the metropolis began to carry passengers, the roads overland being rough and subject to the predations of highwaymen and brigands.

As the interest in sea bathing grew, a stream of people arrived by these sailing hoys, becoming a torrent after the arrival of the first paddle steamship *Thames* in 1815. In 1812 the hoys brought 17,000 visitors to Margate, a figure that had increased by 1836 to 135,000, brought almost entirely by steam packets eager to take advantage of this new activity. The arrival of the railway in 1846 increased this number further.

John Rennie's Pier, constructed of Whitby stone, was completed in 1815. The lighthouse, added in 1829, lasted until it fell in the famous storm of February 1953. It was described at the time as 'an elegant Grecian Doric column, placed on an octagonal base, which serves as a watch house for sailors, and surrounded by a richly ornamented chamber, or lantern, of cast iron.'

Jarvis's Landing Place, which stretched further seaward, was built of oak in 1824. It allowed steamers to berth at low water but was submerged at high tide. Many passengers landed this way until the iron jetty was completed in 1853. The latter was built in the style of the traditional seaside pier, and, when extended, became a major attraction in the town. Sadly it became a victim of fire and bad weather, eventually collapsing in the storm of 1978.

Apart from the period of the two world wars the popularity of Margate remained undiminished. In the years following the last such war, graceful, fast motor ships such as the *Royal Sovereign* and *Royal Daffodil* brought visitors back to Margate in large numbers. Although the town prospered once more, gradually the tastes for seaside holidays changed, and as more people chose the sunshine of Spain, fewer arrived at Margate. In 1966 the General Steam Navigation's summer service to Margate ended, severing a link by sea to London that had existed for centuries. The coal trade to the gasworks ceased at about the same time, and Margate Harbour passed into decline once again. It is still waiting to be rejuvenated.

Ramsgate

Ramsgate became associated with the Cinque Port of Sandwich in about 1353 when the Federation had its greatest power and influence. After that it gradually increased in importance as the haven of Sandwich silted up. Development was slow, however, for a survey carried out in the time of Elizabeth I reported that Ramsgate consisted of twenty-five inhabited houses and possessed fourteen vessels of between 3 and 16 tons. Some seventy men were employed in growing corn and fishing. There remained only a simple haven for many years, but often the need for a harbour of refuge for ships in distress in the Downs was discussed, which led to a proposal in 1744 for Sandwich to be developed to this end. A storm in December 1748 caused those at anchor in the Downs to seek shelter in the little harbour at Ramsgate and, as many ships and lives were saved, the location of the harbour of refuge was altered to Ramsgate.

The construction of the new harbour was a considerable work of engineering and many alterations were necessary before its completion. Begun in 1750, it was largely completed by 1774, but even then the basin needed to be cleared regularly by a drag pulled by horses. Numerous works were carried out by famous engineers such as John Smeaton and Samuel Wyatt, who also built the first lighthouse, but in spite of releasing water through sluices to flush the outer harbour, dredging is still required. Apart from these problems, it fulfilled its purpose as a haven of refuge for ships fleeing before a storm or damaged through contact with the infamous Goodwin Sands, but it was not always easy to enter in bad weather.

King George IV travelled from Ramsgate to Hannover on 25 September 1821, and returned in November. In recognition of the loyalty and welcome shown by the local people he conferred the title 'Royal' on the harbour and an obelisk was erected the following year to record this event.

Ramsgate prospered in the nineteenth century in the same way as Margate, developing as a sea-bathing resort and benefiting from the regular steamer service from London – it being the final port of call. For a long time fishery remained the main occupation of the local populace, and after the Napoleonic Wars a considerable fishing fleet was built up in the town, such that by 1863 fifty smacks were registered at Ramsgate. This figure further increased to 168 by 1906, an increasing number being powered by steam. Sadly the First World War brought an end to this prosperity because almost a third was lost, due to enemy action. Ex-naval steam trawlers replaced some of the lost sailing vessels, but the Second World War again caused a grave depletion of the fleet such that few remained post-war.

In addition to Dover and Margate, the town enjoyed the fame of welcoming home many tired or wounded soldiers from Dunkirk, when 82,000 were landed by ship at the harbour in late May 1940.

The post-war years have seen the enlargement of the harbour to allow cross-Channel ferries to operate from the port. Volkswagen cars were imported from about 1959, with numbers increasing rapidly and ships being built specially for the service, until trade eventually moved to Sheerness in 1994. A large extension was built to the west side of the harbour between 1980 and 1992 enabling large ferries to berth. Those of Sally Line operated from Ramsgate to Dunkirk from 1981 to November 1998. Belgian RMT ferries moved from Dover to Ramsgate in 1994, operating under the name of Oostende Lines. Their ferry *Prins Filip* was the largest vessel ever to enter Ramsgate Harbour, but that service only lasted until 28 February 1997 when the Belgians withdrew from the ferry business, as it had not developed as quickly as it had at Dover, partly because of poor access for heavy vehicles to the port. Nowadays TransEuropa Ferries operate regular crossings to Ostend, profiting from the new access road.

Currently Ramsgate is supporting the construction and maintenance of the major Thanet offshore wind farm. In total 100 turbines are being placed in an area north-east of Ramsgate, near to the Drill Stone buoy.

Dover

The port in Roman times lay in the mouth of the Dour, with the Roman settlement on the rapidly rising west bank. Marked on either side by lighthouses, it was relatively protected from the strong Channel winds and tidal streams.

Dominated by its castle, the town achieved prominence as one of the main Cinque Ports, but the decline suffered by other members was also felt there. Fit inhabitants of the town were called out regularly by the beat of a drum to shovel shingle away from the mouth of the harbour. Both Henry VIII and Elizabeth I made considerable efforts to improve and protect it, but often these well-intentioned changes exacerbated the silting problem. However, since Beckett's martyrdom, pilgrims have crossed in large numbers to visit his shrine at Canterbury. Dover was preferred for the Channel crossing but there are many accounts from the sixteenth century onwards of the trials of such a voyage, should they be attacked by privateers or bad weather, not to mention the hardships of landing on either shore. The exorbitant charges levied by local boatmen for 'faring' or landing people on the beach are regularly mentioned. It being the closest to France, Dover was used as the port of arrival for many of the British and foreign nobility who were no doubt protected from some of these difficulties. One very notable example was Charles II, who returned to Dover to reclaim the throne in 1660.

Dover was also well known for the building of fast cutters of the type used for crossing the Channel, and the local shipbuilders provided similar vessels for the Navy. These fast sailing vessels could equally serve as privateers or revenue cutters.

In the early part of the nineteenth century, the town, in line with others to the north, began to develop as a resort. The shingle bank that had built up along the foreshore was developed in the 1820s to create the prominent Georgian buildings of Marine Parade and Waterloo Crescent. As there were still relatively few crossings by the small steamships, the town remained a relatively quiet and relaxing place, although by virtue of its position it was always defended by a strong military presence.

The arrival of the South Eastern Railway (SER) in 1844 inaugurated the modern era. After that date the number of travellers through the port increased rapidly. The Great Exhibition of 1851 increased this influx from France and Belgium. By 1861 the London, Chatham & Dover Railway (LCDR) also had a station and SER trains were running on to the Admiralty Pier.

In 1844 a report commissioned by the Admiralty on a survey of suitable sites for a harbour of refuge for large warships was published and the site selected was Dover. As a result, the problem of the encroaching shingle was at last overcome by the construction of the Admiralty Pier between 1847 and 1871. The great project of the Admiralty Harbour took from 1899 to 1909 to complete, but its purpose as a base for battleships was never realised due to the strong tides and rough conditions experienced there in strong south-west winds. In the end it became the base for a flotilla of destroyers, submarines and the polyglot fleet of the Dover Patrol, famous for what it achieved with relatively inadequate resources. A later unforeseen benefit was the refuge the harbour offered for the evacuation of Dunkirk.

Outside of the periods of conflict, the Navy rapidly lost interest in the harbour and it was left to the commercial interests of the Harbour Board, founded in 1606, to develop it. The Prince of Wales Pier was opened in 1902 and the Board encouraged the recently formed South Eastern & Chatham Railway Co. to build the Marine Station, which was completed by January 1915. Although it was not used for its original purpose initially, by the time of the Armistice it had allowed the smooth transfer of 1,215,886 wounded from the battlefields of France to trains carrying them to places of care in this country. That same station also accepted evacuees from Dunkirk.

After the Second World War, travellers wished increasingly to take their motor cars abroad, and the last half-century has seen a great expansion in the development and size of car ferries as well as the frequency of sailings. The eastern part of the port has been greatly extended, such that the two drive-on/drive-off berths, built in 1952, have now been increased to eight. The original camber was filled in and the MTB pens demolished to provide a location for a new fruit terminal to replace that situated earlier at the Granville Dock, which with the Wellington Dock and the old Tidal Harbour now accommodate the yacht marina. The port has in recent years catered increasingly for yachtsmen and currently has 397 berths.

A further major development was the conversion of the Marine Station into a cruise terminal in 1996. A second was built four years later, further out along the Admiralty Pier, allowing as many as three cruise ships to be accommodated at any one time, depending on their size. Dover remains a Trust Port committed to further development of this western side of the harbour.

Folkestone

Another settlement with a history going back to Roman times, Folkestone also existed for many years on fishing and agriculture. In 1564 there were apparently seventy fishermen with twenty boats, but even that had dwindled considerably by the end of the century. A small harbour was built, but that suffered from the usual build-up of shingle and, as at Dover, a battle began to keep it open. Coal was imported, but there was much less traffic than at Dover. By 1750, however, most of Kent's ports were involved in the lucrative 'trade' of smuggling, and Folkestone was no exception. The rights of the Cinque portsmen were still remembered, and many seamen along the coast still believed they should import goods without paying taxes. It was stated that Folkestone's smugglers were bold, ruthless, numerous and mostly successful, which could equally be said of those of Dover, Deal, Margate and Ramsgate.

As at other places, Folkestone profited greatly from the arrival of the South Eastern Railway in 1843, who purchased the harbour. After rebuilding it from its derelict state, the SER commenced a regular ferry service to the Continent. The successive railway companies also used the inner harbour as a base for maintaining and repairing their ships.

The fishing industry regained its importance in the late nineteenth century, such that by Edwardian times about 100 luggers worked from the harbour. As at Ramsgate, quite a lot of their catches were carried further by the railway. Dogfish became very popular in the twenties as the country's appetite for fish and chips increased, but nowadays there is little demand for them and cod, turbot and ray species predominate. Eight boats currently fish from the harbour; only one from Hythe and four from Dungeness.

The town became more of a prosperous resort than its neighbour Dover, and also provided more amenities. Officers of the Dover Patrol often travelled to Folkestone during the First World War as there was so little in Dover to entertain them. There was much recrimination when a massive landslip blocked the railway line at the Warren on 20 December 1915, preventing them from reaching Folkestone by rail until after the end of the war.

Although there are barracks at Shorncliffe, Folkestone was never as discernible as a garrison town as Dover. However, during the First World War, many soldiers left from there by ship destined for the Western Front, a considerable number never returning. While they descended the Slope, afterwards named the Road of Remembrance, to the harbour, Ralph Vaughan Williams was inspired to write his moving piece 'A Lark Ascending' from the higher slopes nearby.

After both wars the ferry service to Calais and Boulogne was restored, with a gradual concentration on the latter port. However, Folkestone is more exposed than Dover and can be difficult to enter in heavy weather. Therefore it did not expand as much, and furthermore the depth of the water became a problem as ferries got larger. Sea Containers eventually purchased the harbour from British Rail/Sealink when all their ports were put up for sale, and their subsidiary company, Hoverspeed, commenced a fast catamaran service to Boulogne in 1992. Their craft *Hoverspeed Great Britain* had captured the Blue Riband trophy for fastest crossing of the Atlantic Ocean by a passenger vessel in 1990, before commencing this service.

Sadly, however, the economics for the Folkestone–Boulogne service did not prove viable and the last catamaran crossing occurred in October 2000. Since then Folkestone Harbour has seen few ships apart from the regular fishing boats. A Foxtrot-class Russian submarine was brought in as a visitors' attraction in June 1997 but left in early 2003. It provided an interesting comparison with the *Ocelot* at Chatham.

At the moment the harbour is the subject of re-development plans, having been bought by Roger de Haan, recently of the Saga Insurance Co., from Sea Containers in 2004. Whether the new developments will involve any shipping interests is uncertain at this time.

Broadstairs Harbour has remained relatively unchanged over the last two centuries. As such it is not covered in this work, but this picture, taken around the beginning of the twentieth century, is typical of how most of Kent's harbours would have appeared in the distant past. A stone pier gives shelter to a bay. Sailing barges are discharging into horse-drawn carts and a pulling and sailing lifeboat is drawn up on the pier. Broadstairs Harbour, having escaped major development, remains a peaceful haven.

The Cinque Ports

Cinque Port Seals illustrate the ships of the period

A Hythe Seal   A Sandwich Seal   A Folkestone Seal

A Hastings Seal   Cinque Ports Shield   A Dover Seal

A Winchelsea Seal   A Rye Seal

Note that a vessel with a stern–rudder is illustrated in the Rye seal, a much later development. The fore and after castles also appear more permanent on this vessel.

Cinque Ports Members' Privileges

The Crown gave the Portsmen rights of self-government, allowing them effectively to organise their own affairs. They received:

- **Exemption from tax**. This included lastage (duty by weight), tallage (duty by number), passage (duty on landing) and rivage (a wharf toll). Tallage comes from the French *Taillage* (to cut).

- **Sac and soc**, or full cognizance of all criminal and civil cases within their liberties.

- **Tol and team**. The right to receive tolls to compel a person who held stolen property to name the person from whom he received it.

- **Blodwit and Fledwit**. The right to punish those who shed blood and those who were seized when attempting to flee from justice.

- **Pillory and Tumbrel**. The first was a form of stocks and the latter possibly a ducking stool.

- **Infangentheff and outfangentheff**. The power to imprison and execute felons, whether taken with(in) or with(out) the precincts of the ports.

- **Mundbryce**. The right to try persons for breaches of the King's peace.

- **Waifs and strays**, or the right to appropriate unclaimed or stolen goods abandoned by a thief in flight or cattle not claimed within a year and a day.

- **Flotsam, jetsam or ligan**. The right to seize such material when cast ashore by the sea as 'wreck'. Ligan or lagan refer to goods which lay on the bottom of the sea.

- **Den and Strond**. The right to land and sell fish without fee and dry their nets on others beaches. This applied particularly to Norfolk. In addition, they largely controlled the annual Yarmouth Herring Fair which frequently caused serious conflict with the Portsmen of Norfolk.

- The right to exist as a **Guild** with the power to impose taxes for the common weal.

- The right of assembly in the **Court of Shepway**, west of Hythe. This was later transferred to Dover.

- **Honours at Court**. Representatives of the Cinque Ports were given the privilege originally to carry the canopy protecting the King in the Coronation procession from Westminster Hall to the abbey and to dine at the table at the subsequent banquet.

The Cinque Ports, two 'Antient Towns' and their Limbs

Cinque Port	Corporate Member	Non-corporate member
Hastings 21 ships	Pevensey Seaford	Bulverhythe Petit Higham Hydney Bekesbourne Northeye Grange (Grenche)
Romney 5 ships	**Lydd**	Old Romney Degenmarsh Oswaldstone Promehill
Dover 21 ships	**Folkestone** **Faversham** **Margate**	St John's, Goresend (Birchington) Woodchurch St Peters Kingsdown Ringwould
Sandwich 5 ships	Fordwich **Deal** Walmer **Ramsgate**	Stonor Sarre Brightlingsea (Essex)
Hythe 5 ships		West Hythe
Rye★	**Tenterden**	
Winchelsea★		

The Cinque Ports were legally obliged to provide the King with 57 ships for a period of fifteen days each year. They had also to provide the crews of about twenty-one men for each ship and to cover the costs for this period. The actual numbers seem to have varied. As an example: Folkestone as a limb of Dover had to equip one war vessel, but in 1248 it provided seven vessels for five days. In 1300 only one cock boat for eighteen days was sent and in 1544, one small war vessel with six crew. Margate is understood to have sent fifteen ships with 160 men to help form a fleet raised in 1347 for the Siege of Calais. Dover apparently sent only sixteen ships, but the actual fleet constituted 105 vessels with 2,140 men, far in excess of the normal requirement. Sandwich seems to have sent 22 ships and Winchelsea 21.

Places printed in heavy type indicate the seven ports and seven limbs that form the present Cinque Ports Confederation for ceremonial purposes.

★ Rye and Winchelsea were originally limbs of Hastings but as the latter declined, they achieved 'Port' status themselves but were actually referred to as 'Antient Towns', rather than increasing the number of ports.

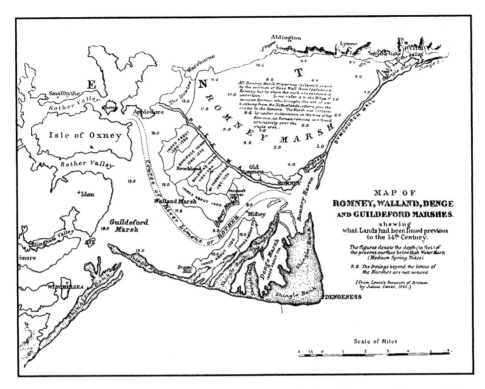

This early map of the 'inning' or reclamation of Romney Marsh shows the protected havens which existed at Romney and Hythe in the Middle Ages. After the River Rother was diverted to Rye by a storm in 1287, Romney was gradually lost to silting. Hythe suffered a similar fate.

This model of an early Cinque Ports ship located in the Science Museum shows the layout of a typical vessel of around AD 1200. These were normal trading vessels which had 'castles' erected at the bow and stern for fighting purposes during their period of service to the Crown. The rudder was more usually located on the 'steer-board' or starboard side. Later it was moved to the stern.

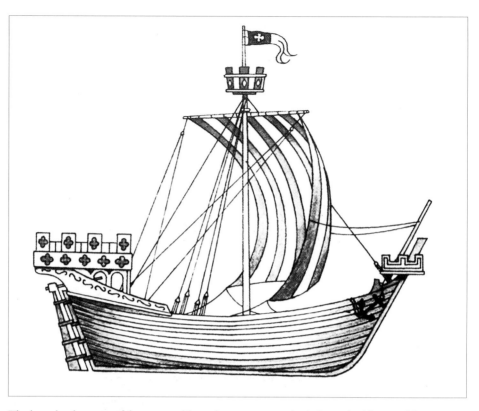

The later development of the stern rudder and permanent castles is shown in this cog of the thirteenth and fourteenth centuries. It is similar to that shown earlier on the Rye seal. (E.H.H. Archibald, also header page)

The role of the Lord Warden, once powerful, is now purely honorary. Appointed in 2004, the current Lord Warden, Admiral the Lord Boyce GCB, OBE, was installed at a session of the Grand Court of Shepway at Dover College on 12 April 2005. Lord Boyce joined the Navy in 1961 and trained as a submariner. After commanding various submarines and the frigate HMS *Brilliant*, he was promoted to flag rank in 1991. He became First Sea Lord in 1998 and Chief of the Defence Staff in 2001. (Admiral Lord Boyce)

2
Chatham and Rochester

The original main gate of Chatham Dockyard, shown here at the beginning of the twentieth century, remains relatively unchanged today. It was built of brick in 1720. Enormous streams of men would flow through this gate at the beginning and end of the working day during the period the dockyard was operating. (Wrench Series)

The Commissioner's House as seen from the garden. Built in the Queen Anne style in 1703-04 it has a grand interior, the rooms having heavily panelled walls and painted ceilings. It is reputedly the oldest surviving complete naval building in Britain. The Commissioner had overall responsibility for the dockyard, being appointed by the Board of Admiralty. (A.L.)

Upnor Castle was built for the defence of the Medway between 1559 and 1567 to a design by Sir Richard Lee. Although occupying a prominent position and being improved in 1600, it achieved very little in military terms, failing to repel the Dutch incursion into the Medway in 1667. Until recent times it was a munitions store, 5,206 barrels of powder being held there as early as 1691. (A.L.)

The covered building slips of Chatham Dockyard, seen from the river, starting with No. 3 at the extreme right and moving upwards to No. 7. No. 3 slip was covered over in 1838. Many ships were built on No. 7 slip including the battleships HMS *Agamemnon* (launched 1879), *Prince of Wales* (1901) and later a number of submarines. (A.L.)

The most famous ship to be built at Chatham is Nelson's flagship HMS *Victory*. She was built in the Old Single Dock, which was later rebuilt and now holds the destroyer HMS *Cavalier*. Work commenced on 26 August 1759 and she was launched on 7 May 1765. She was also very largely rebuilt at Chatham in the years 1800 to 1803, not long prior to the Battle of Trafalgar.

The Royal National Lifeboat Institution also has a museum in the Chatham Historic Dockyard. Amongst the numerous boats on display is the 35ft pulling and sailing lifeboat *Lizzie Porter*, dating from 1909, which served at Holy Island and North Sunderland. (A.L.)

The earliest ship to be preserved at Chatham is the Osprey-class sloop HMS *Gannet*, which dates from the era when both sail and steam were combined for propulsion. This vessel was launched at Sheerness in 1878 and has enjoyed a long and interesting career. Her naval service ended in 1895 and afterwards she spent many years in a training role, firstly as HMS *President* (1903) and later as TS *Mercury* (1914). After retirement in 1968, she was given to the Maritime Trust and was eventually brought to Chatham in June 1987 for restoration. Nowadays, after a great deal of work, she appears as she did in 1885. (A.L.)

Another vessel of interest which has spent many years on the Medway is the steam paddle tug *John H. Amos*. She was built in 1931 for service on the Tees. Unlike *TID 164*, also moored at Chatham, she is not a naval tug but is reminiscent of those like the *Cracker* which served at Sheerness Dockyard. *John H. Amos* belongs to the Medway Maritime Trust and has recently been placed on a pontoon to allow restoration to commence. (A.L.)

HMS *Challenger* was built at Chatham in 1931, initially to serve as a fishery investigation vessel. After 1933 she became a survey ship, charting many different parts of the world from the English coastline to the West Indies, Persian Gulf and Labrador. She was finally broken up at Dover in 1954. (Shipping Wonders of the World)

Although not built at Chatham, the dockyard is fortunate enough to have the last destroyer to see service in the Second World War. HMS *Cavalier* is the sole survivor of a large group of 'C'-class vessels. She was completed by J. Samuel White at Cowes in 1944 and came to Chatham for preservation ten years ago. Recently a memorial to all destroyers lost during the last war has been placed next to this ship.

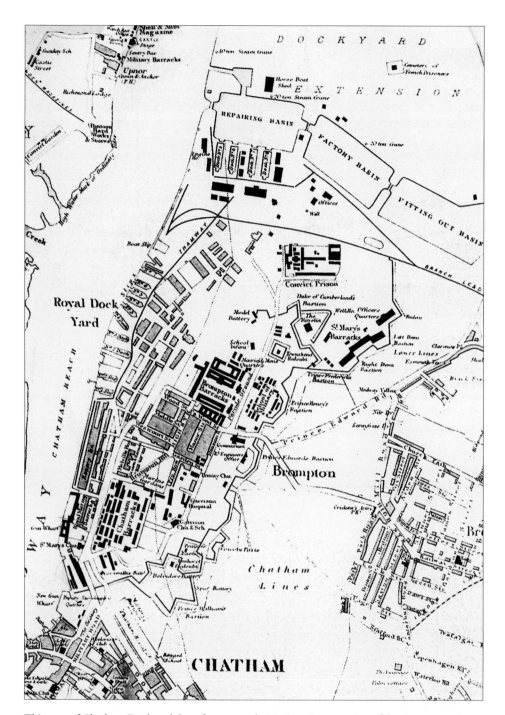

This map of Chatham Dockyard dates from around 1885. A major extension of the site occurred between 1862 and 1885 which increased more than fourfold the area of the dockyard. The extended site included three repairing, building and fitting-out basins which ran along the length of the earlier St Mary's Creek. A considerable amount of convict labour was involved, as indicated by the prison within the site.

HM Submarines built at Chatham 1908–1967

Name	Launch date	Tonnage	Fate
C.17-C.20	1908-09	280	Sold to be broken up, 1919-21
C.33-C.34	1910	280	C.33 lost 4.8.15; C.34 sunk by U-52 on 21.7.17
D.7-D.8	1911	550	Broken up at Porstmouth, 1921
E.1 (ex. D.9)	1912	660	Destroyed in Helsingfors 4.1918 to avoid capture
E.2 (ex-D.10)	1912	660	Broken up at Malta in 1921
E.7	1913	660	Destroyed in 1915 by explosives at Dardenelles
E.8	1913	660	Scuttled with E.1 at Helsingfors
E.12	1914	660	Broken up at Malta in 1921
E.13	1914	660	Stranded September 1915 on the coast of Denmark, interned
F.1	1915	353	Broken up at Portsmouth Dockyard 1920
G.1-G.5	1915-16	700	G.1-G.3 scrapped Sunderland 1920-21, G.4 and G.5 broken up 1928 and 1922 at Newport, Monmouth
R.1-R.4	1918	410	R.1-R.3 broken up 1923, R.4 in 1934
X.1	1923	2,780	Experimental, broken up at Pembroke in 1936
Oberon	1926	1,311	Broken up in 1945 at Rosyth
Odin	1928	1,475	Sunk June 1940 by Italian destroyer *Strale* near Taranto
Parthian	1929	1,475	Presumed mined in Southern Adriatic 11.8.43
Rainbow	1930	1,475	Torpedoed off Calabria c.19.10.40
Grampus	1936	1,520	Depth-charged off Augusta, Sicily, lost 24.6.40
Seal	1938	1,520	Captured 2.5.1940 by German aircraft in Kattegatt. Became U-boat. Scuttled 1945. Later scrapped
Sturgeon	1932	670	To Netherlands Navy as *Zeehond* (1943-45), scrapped at Granton, 1947
Swordfish	1931	670	Lost by unknown cause off Ushant, 16.11.40
Seahorse	1932	670	Depth-charged in Heligoland Bight, lost 7.1.40
Starfish	1933	670	Depth-charged in Heligoland Bight, lost 9.1.40

Name	Launch date	Tonnage	Fate
Shark	1934	670	Depth-charged off Skudesnes, lost 6.7.40
Snapper	1934	670	Lost by unknown cause in Bay of Biscay c.12.2.41
Sunfish	1936	670	Lent to Russia as B.1 in 1944. Lost 27.7.44
Sterlet	1937	670	Depth-charged in the Skagerrak, lost 16.4.40
Splendid	1942	715	Depth-charged off Corsica and scuttled, 21.4.43
Sportsman	1942	715	Lent to France as Sibylle in 1952. Lost 23.9.52
Shalimar	1943	715	Scrapped at Troon in 1950
Tigris	1939	1,090	Lost by unknown cause in Gulf of Naples, 10.3.43
Torbay	1940	1,090	Broken up at Briton Ferry 1945-46
Tradewind	1942	1,090	Broken up at Charlestown in 1955
Trenchant	1943	1,090	Broken up at Faslane in 1963
Thermopylae	1945	1,090	Broken up at Troon in 1971
Turpin	1944	1,090	Transferred to Israeli Navy 1965, renamed Leviathan
Umpire	1941	540	Sunk in error off the Wash on 19.7.41
Una	1941	540	Broken up at Llanelly in 1949
Acheron	1947	1,120	Broken up at Newport in 1972
Oberon	1959	1,610	Sold to Egyptian Navy, 1987
Onslaught	1960	1,610	Paid off in 1990
Ocelot	1962	1,610	Preserved at Chatham Historic Dockyard
Ojibwa	1964	1,610	For Royal Canadian Navy. Decommissioned May 1998
Onondaga	1965	1,610	For Royal Canadian Navy. Decommissioned July 2000
Okanagan	1966	1,610	For Royal Canadian Navy. Decommissioned September 1998

The Rothesay-class frigate HMS *Yarmouth* approaches the entrance lock to the dockyard towards the end of her career. This 2,380-ton vessel was built by John Brown in 1960 and was the first of her class to enter service. In 1976 she came into the yard for repairs to her bow sustained in collisions with Icelandic gunboats during the Cod Wars. Later she served in the Falklands Campaign and rescued survivors from HMS *Sheffield* and HMS *Ardent*. She was sunk as a target in 1987.

The Leander-class frigate HMS *Hermione* (F58) was the last naval vessel to leave Chatham Dockyard in the summer of 1983, bringing to an end nearly 400 years of naval shipbuilding and maintenance at the port. The *Hermione* was commissioned in 1969 and paid off in 1992.

Although Chatham Dockyard became a museum in 1985, links with the Royal Navy were re-established in May 1999 when Navy Days were recreated in a limited way. Both foreign and British warships were invited to attend as well as a range of diverse smaller craft. This view from the bow of the French minesweeper *Cassiopée* shows visitors boarding HMS *Exeter*. (A.L.)

The Sheffield-class destroyer HMS *Exeter* (D89) leaves from the Bullnose at Chatham Dock entrance lock in May 1999 after the completion of her Navy Days visit. She was built by Swan Hunter in 1980. In June 2009 HMS *Argyll* came to Chatham for the first of the National Armed Forces Day's celebrations. (A.L.)

Moving to the Port of Rochester where commercial shipping has held sway, one company with a history stretching back more than a century was the London Rochester Trading Co., later to become Crescent Shipping. Starting with sailing barges, they later progressed to steel barges and motor coasters, all with distinctive terracotta-coloured hulls. They had their head office at Canal Road, Rochester, and their own shipyard at Frindsbury, Strood, from where this barge, the *Rohoy*, was launched in 1966. (Alan Jenner)

Another Crescent barge, the *Loach*, is seen off Strood Yard looking towards Rochester Bridge and the castle. The 31m *Loach* was built by Cubow at Woolwich in 1968 to load about 300 tons of general cargo. *Lobe*, *Locator* and *Lodella* were similar. Strood Yard is now owned by Denton Ship Repairers Ltd. (Crescent Shipping)

Above: Crescent purchased their first motor coaster before the Second World War. In later years they progressed alphabetically with *Dominence, Faience, Gardience, Halcience, Jubilence* etc. The 959-ton *Nascence*, shown here, built to a low-profile 'sea snake' design, was completed in 1978 and remained with the company until 1992. After becoming part of the Hay's Wharf group, Crescent Shipping was sold off and ceased trading some years ago.

Left: Crescent also operated their own tugs, firstly in the river and later at the commercial Chatham Dock. They also had original names. The *Lashette* and her sister *Shovette* were built at Strood in 1971 and 1974 and were the last of Crescent's tugs. Both were sold in 1998. (A.L.)

Telephone: CHATHAM 91.

The New Medway Steam Packet Co. Limited.

DIRECTORS:
C. WILLIS.
G. G. WATSON.
E. H. ELLIOTT.
S. J. SHIPPICK.

SECRETARY,
E. SCOONES.

280, High Street,
Rochester, Sept 28th 1924.

This page: The New Medway Steam Packet Co. was incorporated in December 1919, acquiring the assets of the Medway Steam packet Company of 1881, which was a successor to the company of the same title of 1837. The latter was originally formed to link Chatham with Sheerness by water. Under the leadership of its ambitious managing director Sidney Shippick, the New Medway Steam Packet Co. grew appreciably in the 1930s. He adopted the name of Queen Line of Steamers in 1924, progressing from offering outings to Southend to longer trips to Dover and the French ports of Calais and Boulogne.

QUEEN LINE of PLEASURE STEAMERS

FAST SALOON STEAMERS.
NEW MEDWAY STEAM PACKET CO., LTD.

From MARGATE JETTY to

C A L A I S (Sundays to Thursdays)
11.15 a.m. Allowing about 2¼ hours in Calais.
8/6 Return.

D O V E R (Mondays & Wednesdays)
11.30 a.m.
3/- Return.

Afternoon Sea Trips
To GOODWIN SANDS,
GULL LIGHTSHIP &
EDINBURGH CHANNEL,
Sundays, Tuesdays, Thursdays, Fridays and Saturdays, 2.40 p.m.
FARE: **2/-**

For further particulars, see Handbills and Posters, or apply:
MR. F. G. FRIGHT, at Queen Line Offices, Margate Jetty. 'Phone 1430.

All Trips weather and other circumstances permitting and subject to alteration without notice.

BOULOGNE—
FRIDAYS, AUGUST 16th, 23rd & 30th } 10 a.m.
SPECIAL DAY TRIPS.
Allowing nearly Three hours ashore. **10/6** RETURN. Children 6/6.

LUNCHEONS, DINNERS & REFRESHMENTS ON BOARD.
NEW MEDWAY STEAM PACKET Co., Ltd., High Street, ROCHESTER.

Captains Philip Kitto, left, and Tom Aldis served long periods with the New Medway Steam Packet Co. Both served in the Navy throughout the war. Tom Aldis enjoyed, or rather endured, a rather eventful career in peacetime as well as during the war. Gaining the DSC at Dunkirk aboard the *Royal Sovereign*, he survived the sinking of that ship off South Wales in December 1940. Another ship was sunk when he was serving as its pilot for the Mulberry Harbour at Arromanches after the D-Day invasion. (Medway Studios)

The steel paddle steamer *Princess of Wales* was built in 1896 by Craggs of Middlesborough and used on the Rochester to Southend service. In June 1917 she was requisitioned by the Admiralty, later renamed *Padua* and employed on the naval Medway ferry service until April 1920. A charter to Scotland followed, where she sank in 1927. She was broken up the following year. (H.W. Herbert, Chatham)

After the First World War the New Medway Co. purchased two Ascot-class naval minesweepers and converted them to a passenger-carrying role. Named the *Queen of Thanet* and the *Queen of Kent*, they were the most important units of the fleet until the arrival of the *Queen of the Channel* in 1935. Both survived the later war and the *Queen of Kent* is here seen off the Essex coast not long before she was sold for service on the Solent. Both were broken up at Dover at the end of their lives. (World Ship Society)

Arguably the most famous of the Medway steamers is the still surviving *Medway Queen*, built at Troon in 1924. Operated on the Rochester–Southend route for a large part of her life, she also worked to Herne Bay before the war. Her master for many years post-war was Captain Len Horsham. A Dunkirk veteran, she has been the object of preservation efforts for many years. It now seems that those who persevered have been successful and that this noteworthy little paddler will be rebuilt.

Although the New Medway Co. has long disappeared, the public can still travel down the Medway aboard the preserved coal-burning paddle steamer *Kingswear Castle* built in 1924. It is still occasionally possible to cross to Southend for a day out and this picture was taken on such a voyage. (A.L.)

John Megoran has been master of the *Kingswear Castle* since she arrived in the Medway twenty-five years ago from the River Dart. He is also business manager for the vessel and looks after her care and maintenance over the winter period. He is very proud of the reliability of the ship, which provides many excursions during the summer months from Rochester Pier or Chatham Historic Dockyard. (A.L.)

Leaving the Medway. Representing the many ships that have carried wood pulp and other forest products to the Medway for many years is the 4,400-ton Swedish vessel *Noren*. She is seen outward bound in Short Reach after leaving Crown Wharf at Rochester. (A.L.)

3

SHEERNESS

A view of the Bluetown area of Sheerness, drawn around 1830. The engraving was made from the site of the entrance to the pier first built in 1835. A Wesleyan chapel is situated to the right and the Jolly Sailor Inn, still open today, and Commercial Hotel, later the Royal Fountain Inn, are in the centre. Nowadays the high dockyard wall considerably restricts the view. (T.M. Baynes, Geo. Virtue)

A view of the interior of the dockyard in the final days of the Royal Navy. The large quadrangular storehouse at the rear, at one time the largest brick building in the country, was demolished as part of the development of the commercial port, only the clock tower being preserved. It had iron joists and window frames and could contain 30,000 tons of stores. (Eric de Maré)

Above: An aerial view of Sheerness Dockyard from about 1960 after the Royal Navy had departed and before the commercial development of the yard had commenced. The large quadrangular store is again visible to the right of the picture. Three dry docks lead off the Great Basin in the centre foreground. The only recognisable feature nowadays is the Boat Store, visible at the top centre.

Left: Ship's figureheads were a prominent feature of naval dockyards in the past. That of the *Poitiers* is shown on display at Sheerness around 1996. Built at Upnor in 1809, she was a 3rd rate ship of the line having a tonnage of 1,765 by builders' measurement. The *Poitiers* was broken up in 1857, possibly at Sheerness. Other figureheads held at the dockyard include *Goliath*, *Chesapeake* and *Forte*, but none are now on display. (A.L.)

The Boat Store at Sheerness, constructed in 1860, is the earliest multi-storey, iron-framed building in existence and is therefore of great architectural importance. It measures 210ft in length, 135ft in width and is 53ft high. It is currently Grade 1 listed. (A.L.)

Ridham Dock lies on the Swale just east of the Kingsferry Bridges. It was originally commenced in 1913 for Frank, later Edward, Lloyd, but on completion in 1917 it was taken over by the Admiralty as a salvage depot. After that war, timber and wood pulp for papermaking were discharged there, reaching the Sittingbourne and Kemsley mills by means of a light railway. In 1948 the owners became Bowaters Lloyd. After the paper mill closed trade diversified. Bretts now have a plant receiving aggregates and Ridham Sea Terminals handle various cargoes in the remaining part. (A.L.)

There was no bridge across the Swale until 1860 when the Queen's Bridge was opened, but by 1862 both rail and road vehicles could cross. This single bascule lifting bridge was opened in 1904 with tolls levied on vehicles crossing until July 1929. This bridge, at the place of the earlier King's Ferry, allowed ships to pass through to Ridham Dock. Here the *Gunvor Maersk* passes the bridge assisted by the motor tug *Mamba* in July 1953. In October of the following year the bridge was closed for five days after being struck by the *Louisa Gorthon*. (Gaselees)

The bascule bridge was replaced by a horizontal lift bridge in 1960. The railway has precedence and ships must book a bridge lift which avoids the half-hourly trains. In this recent view MV *Salix* passes through on her way to Grovehurst Jetty. At the rear is the new Sheppey Crossing road bridge which was completed in July 2006. Any possibility of isolation of the island by a ship damaging the bridge is now avoided. (A.L.)

The BP oil refinery at the Isle of Grain was begun in the early 1950s and opened by the new tanker *British Sailor* in 1954. It was gradually extended until about 1960 by which time it had eight tanker berths and one smaller coaster pier. This view, taken around 1960, shows the refinery near the final stage of expansion when it was capable of accepting the largest tankers afloat. (Fotoflite)

This painting by Ian Boyd shows Knights' tugs *Kite* and *Kent* assisting the BP tanker *British Courage* to leave her berth at the Isle of Grain. It is a nostalgic reminder of the refinery, which closed in 1984. The tug *Kent* is preserved in Chatham Dock by the South Eastern Tug Society, who have kindly allowed this reproduction of their 1997 Christmas card.

Only No.1 berth remained in use at Grain after the closure of the refinery, and that purely for the storage and distribution of aviation fuel. As another reminder of the past, the tanker *Sea Horse* draws alongside with a cargo from Libya in 1994. This vessel was previously the BP tanker *British Security*. (A.L.)

Many developments are repeated in the course of time. It was perhaps no surprise therefore that BP renewed its interests in the Isle of Grain by constructing a natural gas terminal in 2005. This view shows the LNG tanker *British Trader* entering the Medway on 2 April 2009. She was the hundredth vessel to call at the new berth. A second is nearing completion at the present time. (A.L.)

Part of the land occupied by the Grain refinery was taken over by the Thamesport container terminal which opened in May 1990. In 1993, 144,000 containers were handled. The installation catered initially for the large Evergreen Marine Corporation of Taiwan. Other lines such as Hapag-Lloyd and NYK quickly followed. Here the French CMA container ship *Ville de Libra* is manoeuvred alongside in October 1995. Ken Goodsell waits to take the lines. (A.L.)

Crane driver Barry Wakefield worked originally at Tilbury Dock. Here he demonstrates how he locates the correct containers to be removed from the ship. This appears a difficult task to the uninitiated as ships calling at Thamesport nowadays can carry as many as 6,000 TEU (20ft equivalent units). (A.L.)

An impressive view of the ship is obtained from the crane cabin. The boom must reach across thirteen containers on the *Ville de Libra*. This 37,000-ton vessel was typical of the container ships of the 1990s. Nowadays the breadth of ships has increased to allow up to eighteen containers to be carried abreast, and the crane booms have had to be extended accordingly. (A.L.)

A view of the yard at Thamesport in its early days when it was owned and operated by Robin McLeod and Maritime Transport Services Ltd. It is now part of Hutchison Port Holdings, who also own Felixstowe. Automatic travelling cranes and tugs are used to move the containers rather than straddle carriers. (A.L.)

As one ship leaves Thamesport, another arrives. In pleasant summer weather the *Al Mirqab* is swung by the tugs before making fast alongside. This vessel belongs to the United Arab Shipping Corporation of Kuwait, whose ships are also regular callers at Thamesport. (A.L.)

Present-day container ships can be very large. Typical of the latest generation and the largest to visit the Medway is the 338m *Hyundai Mercury*, seen here outward bound passing Garrison Point. Built in Korea in 2008, she is close to 100,000 gross tons and draws 14m when fully loaded. (A.L.)

Another company which occupies the site of the earlier BP refinery on the Isle of Grain is Foster Yeoman. A large number of the concrete sections for the Channel Tunnel were made there. Bulk carriers regularly deliver large quantities of road stone from Glensanda in Scotland for distribution to other berths in the Thames and around the coast. The *Yeoman Brook* was a regular caller in the 1990s but has now been replaced by the *Yeoman Bridge* and *Yeoman Bontrup*. (A.L.)

Other bulk carriers call regularly at Sheerness. Gearbulk ships bring wood pulp and other products from Brazil and Chile to No.2 berth. The MV *Harefield* of 28,000 tons, seen here approaching Sheerness, is typical of these vessels, all of which have self-discharging gantry cranes. Most Gearbulk callers have 'Arrow' names; i.e. *Teal Arrow*, *Toucan Arrow* and *Wren Arrow*. (A.L.)

Kingsnorth Power Station dates from the early 1970s and has an output of close to 2,000 megawatts. It is coal fired but has the capability to burn oil as well. Colliers deliver coal regularly to the power station jetty but oil is pumped ashore at Oakham Ness, which can also supply Grain Power Station. Now under the ownership of E-ON, the replacement of both stations is being considered at this time. (A.L.)

Three colliers, the *Lord Citrine*, *Lord Hinton* and *Sir Charles Parsons*, each with a capacity of some 23,000 tons, have supplied Kingsnorth from the mid-1980s. Since the *Lord Citrine* was sold more than ten years ago, a number of self-discharging vessels have been chartered as required to guarantee the required deliveries of coal. (A.L.)

Returning to the earlier post-war years of Sheerness Dockyard, the Admiralty operated a number of tugs of varying power and performance. The *Tryphon* was one of the larger Assurance-class of vessels of 630 tons built in 1942. After her naval service she was sold for commercial use at Sheerness and renamed *Melanie Fair*. A large tug for her day, she had a bollard pull (bp) of 13½ tons, which is modest by today's standards.

Besides the naval tugs, the firm of J.P. Knight was well known for many years as a tug operator on both the Thames and Medway. In a flashback to the 1950s, the crew of the *Kestrel* of 1955 are, from left: Les Mills, Sid Wood, Michael Komenda, Bill Scott, George Maple, Charlie Harold and Dick Bailey. The eighth member of the crew, seaman/cook Albert Clifton, was below. (Ron Kite collection)

Knights were a Rochester firm, providing tugs adequate to tow barges up to Maidstone but also those powerful enough to berth the largest tankers at the Isle of Grain. The *Kite* of 1951 was employed on the larger ships until her sale for scrap in 1982. (Ray Harrison)

Knights' Tugs Serving the Medway

When I started work in 1942 at the age of fourteen, I was mate of the MV *The Flame* with my father. *The Flame* had been commandeered by the Government and was engaged in carrying ammunition to HM ships at Sheerness from Upnor and Grain Armament Depots. Knights' tugs also working there were MT *Kathleen* (Captain Herbert), MT *Keston* (Captain J. Mizzen), ST *Kennet* (Captain Herbert), ST *Kenley* (Captain S. Cornell) and sometimes ST *Kite* (Captain Pope).

My cousin, Stan Cornell (Jerry), had joined Knights before the war, after having been mate with his father in the MV *Atrato* of London Rochester Trading Company. Later he had the *Keston* and *Kite*. He is shown on the right in the wheelhouse of the *Kite* in the picture above, together with a pilot.

The wood pulp ships did not berth at Reed's Mills but on buoys in the river at Rochester and worked overside into lighters which were then towed up river. The tugs would meet the ships downriver and escort them to their moorings. Manoeuvring them round Chatham Point was the most skilful job, as was swinging the ships in Limehouse Reach.

After the war, London Rochester had their own tugs and motor barges, so Knights lost most of the lighterage work on the Medway, and by the 1950s they only had Cory's Coal to Snodland and Maidstone. The London Rochester Trading Co. had the delightful names of *Dragette* (50 tons) and *Enticette* (108 tons) for their larger tugs and *Coaxette*, *Luggette*, *Pullette* and *Snatchette* for the smaller vessels.

Thomas Watson also had their own tug and the oil depots were being served by the MT *Crowstone* and several motor tank barges. Luckily the advent of the Kent Oil Refinery, and later Sheerness Docks, saved the day for Knights.

Before L. R. T. C. had their own tugs, Knights also towed their craft to London, the tug from the Medway would meet the tug from London and change over their tows in Sea Reach. I do not think that Knights did much work for Bowaters (at Ridham) as this was usually done by Gaselees. I always considered Knights' tugs to be very smart and well maintained vessels. (Personal account by Duncan Francis of Lairg, Sutherland.)

The older and newer generations of Medway tugs are seen here together. The *Kennet* and *Knighton* were the last of J.P. Knights' single-screw tugs to serve at Sheerness. Alongside the *Kennet* is the *Lady Morag* built in 1983, one of the first Japanese-built vessels with fully rotating 'Z' drive units which allow much greater manoeuvrability. She is still in service as the *Svitzer Morag*. (A.L.)

A group of Howard Smith tug crew members gathered together in 1998. At the rear are, from left: Trevor Edgley, Steve Goodyear, Paul Kite, Trevor Beck and David Bowles. On the front row are: Mick Kelly, Peter Riddle and Barry Fullager. (Ron Kite)

David Brown knew the *Kennet* well having spent sixteen years as her master. He has seen many changes during a long career with the Thames and Medway tugs. Starting in 1966 with 'Sun' tugs on the Thames, he moved to the Medway in 1972, becoming master of the *Kemsing* at age twenty-four in 1975. In 1991 he came ashore as office manager for Knights, who soon sold the concern to Howard Smith of Australia. He now manages both the Thames and Medway operations for Svitzers. (A.L.)

A relatively recent arrival at Sheerness is the *Svitzer Trimley*. She is seen here moving out to swing the incoming container ship *Tokyo Express* prior to berthing at Thamesport. Previously stationed at Felixstowe, the 3,500hp *Svitzer Trimley* has a bollard pull (bp) of 43 tons, relatively modest compared to her two companions *Svitzer Warden* and *Svitzer Harty* which are of 70 tons bp. (A.L.)

A very important trade to Sheerness is the import of motor vehicles. Car carriers of various sizes call frequently, as exemplified by the *Carmen*, one of the largest types of around 55,000 gross tons. Their design does not change a great deal and the *Carmen*, although built in 1982, is similar in appearance to more modern varients. Wallenius AB name their vessels after famous operas. (A.L.)

Passenger Ferries once made regular visits to the Medway. A Queenborough–Flushing service operated in the early years of the twentieth century and the rail link to Port Victoria on the Isle of Grain allowed ferries to operate from there. Much later the Olau Line renewed the service to Vlissingen from Sheerness, eventually building the super ferries *Olau Hollandia* and *Olau Britannia*. Sadly, they were not viable in the long term and their last sailing occurred on 18 May 1994. (John Gurton)

Two views taken from ships arriving in the Medway in 1994. Here the MV *Haskerland* heads inwards past Kingsnorth Power Station towards her berth in Chatham Dock. She is carrying wood pulp from Sydney, Nova Scotia. (A.L.)

An earlier design of Cuban reefer dating from 1977, the *Oceano Artico* is assisted alongside at Sheerness by Howard Smith's tugs. She has arrived from Cuenfuegos to deliver 685 tons of grapefruit and is making a further call at Rotterdam. (A.L.)

While most commercial ships are nowadays designed for maximum cargo capacity and scant attention is given to appearance, fruit ships have remained the most elegant and streamlined of vessels. Unfortunately their appearance is now modified by the carriage of numerous containers on deck. This picture of Cool Carriers' *Swan Bay* was taken before containerisation of fruit became commonplace. (A.L.)

Medway Ports employs thirty-six pilots to ensure that vessels navigate the river and approach channels safely. They normally board and land at the Warps, North-East Spit, or the Sunk, depending on the draught and length of the vessel. Here a pilot leaves a ship off Garrison Point as the master has an exemption certificate for the approaches. (A.L.)

After the pilot boards, the master sometimes leaves the bridge to get some rest. MV *Nordic Amanda* is inward bound for Crown Wharf, Rochester. Her pilot, Glyn Wintle, originally comes from the Medway Towns. After a period deep-sea, he trained as a pilot for the Thames and later transferred to the Medway. (A.L.)

Inward bound from Hamburg, the MV *Salix* is heading for Grovehurst Jetty with a cargo of 3,000 tons of gypsum. Here her master, Vladimir Lipçenko (left), and Medway pilot Andy Weale, keep watch in the Prince's Channel. Andy joined at Sheerness just after Trinity House handed over pilotage to the harbour authority in 1988. He was previously on cross-Channel ferries. (A.L.)

All traffic entering or leaving the Medway is monitored by the VTS (Vessel Traffic Management System) team at Garrison Point, Sheerness, led by assistant harbourmaster Kevin Beacon. The modern office accommodation is built on a Victorian fort and enjoys excellent views of the river and passing ships. (A.L.)

Derek Kemp has been a member of the VTS team for twenty-one years, having previously served in the Royal Navy as Chief Yeoman. TV screens allow visual views of almost every part of the river and radar displays cover all important areas of the Thames Estuary. (A.L.)

Inward bound is Swedish master Per Elmlund aboard his 5,500-ton self-discharging vessel *Sunnanhav*. No stranger to the Medway, he is interested in the history of the region. The ship has twelve crew; the master and chief engineer are Swedish and the remainder Polish. (A.L.)

In charge ashore is Cathryn Spain, harbourmaster at Sheerness since April 2009. She joined Medway Ports after eighteen years of experience with P&O containers and Hoverspeed. She has overall responsibility for the harbour, while Marine Services are supervised by deputy harbourmaster Guy Peto. (A.L.)

4

WHITSTABLE

Seen at the entrance to Whitstable Harbour prior to the First World War are the brigantines *Raven* (left) and *Dolly Varden*. The former was built at Prince Edward Island in 1873 and the latter at Bideford in 1871. Both were owned at Whitstable. The *Dolly Varden* was sunk in November 1917 by a German submarine after delivering coal to Dieppe.

Whitstable Harbour.   Valentine's Series

A view of the inner harbour from the late Victorian period shows how busy the port was in those days. The brigantine on the south quay is believed to be the 200-ton *Mary A. Mckay*, built at Prince Edward Island in 1864 for Whitstable owners. (Valentine's series)

Whitstable has also attracted its share of bathers and sun-worshippers, although not on the scale of the resorts further east. The main beaches are located in the newer suburb of Tankerton, but Reeves Beach is situated just to the west of the harbour. George Reeves, a relative of William Reeves, for whom the beach is named, provided meals for eighty children for three months in the freezing winter of 1897. This view is along Sea Wall towards that beach. Stone House is still in existence. (W.J. Cox)

After Whitstable Urban District Council purchased the harbour from British Railways in 1958 trade improved and after the West Quay was built in 1966 it became very busy. Crescent Shipping's 200-ton *Gillation* was built at Rochester in 1964 and is of almost exactly the same size as the *Mary A. McKay* and *Raven* shown earlier. Bretts earlier tarmac plant is in the background to the left. (Duncan Francis)

Whitstable Oyster Fishery

Andy Riches, below, fishes all year round for oysters with his boat *Misty* from Whitstable. Two varieties are found from about a mile offshore, the relatively recently introduced and farmed Pacific 'Rock' oysters, and the Whitstable 'Native' ones which have been fished for upwards of two millennia. The two types of oyster differ in shape, the Native being much flatter, and they differ also in taste. Both are obtained by a process of dredging. In the days of sail the dredge was about 2ft wide and comprised an iron bar dragged along the bottom which lifted the oysters and directed them into a 'bag' attached to the rear of the dredge. The *Gamecock* (F76) shown at the head of this chapter is typical of that type and is still in existence. A motor fishing boat such as *Misty* will now pull a dredge 6ft wide with a rake instead of a bar. The rake draws up far less debris from the bottom than the flat iron bar.

Using this method Andy catches about 100,000 Rock oysters a year and about 20,000 Natives. The former can be fished for all year round, but the natives are left undisturbed from May to August, when there is no 'r' in the month. As this is their breeding season they become weaker and smaller and they are left to reproduce in peace.

The oysters, once caught, are placed in tanks filled with filtered salt water circulated at a constant temperature as shown below. This process cleans them of any internal bacteria or other impurities. Most oysters caught are clean enough to be eaten direct from the sea but the cleaning process is strictly followed according to Government demands and monitored by local council tests on a monthly basis.

Andy has been fishing for thirty-seven years, starting from Whitstable in 1977. He has gradually transferred from trawling for white fish to total dedication to the oysters, all of which are taken by the Whitstable Oyster Co. and sold at restaurants in the town. He says little has changed in the method of fishing over the years, except that he now has a motorised winch to haul in the dredge and he uses satellite navigation to locate the oysters.

Andy Riches' boat *Misty* falls into the under 10m class. A plastic owl is attached to the top of the winch in an attempt to discourage scavenging birds. (A.L.)

Cockle boats also work successfully from Whitstable, bringing in about 20 tons a day in the summer season, but the period is now restricted. Quantities of bass and thornback ray are caught locally. Some 62 tons of white fish were landed at the harbour in 2008. Such catches are sold to local, regional and export markets. Here the trawlers *Millennia* and *Charlie Boy* are shown alongside the quay. (A.L.)

Steve Norris has been sailing his barge *Greta* out of Whitstable for some years in summertime. *Greta* was built at Brightlingsea in 1892 and is a veteran of Dunkirk. On most summer days Steve and his crew takes up to twelve passengers out to the Red Sands fort and the Kentish Flats wind farm. He also competes in a number of barge matches around the coast with considerable success. (A.L.)

Steve's dog Alfie also lives aboard. After sleeping rough for some time he was given his own kennel a year or so ago. (A.L.)

Steve's barge *Greta* approaches Whitstable Harbour entrance on a fine day. Access is only possible for three hours either side of high water. Bretts tarmac plant on the east quay is the most prominent feature. (A.L.)

Whitstable Harbour has not developed to the extent of other Kentish harbours. The west quay, shown in the lower part of this photograph, the only recent extension, was initially used by Westland Imports for fresh vegetables, but many cargoes have been unloaded there, latterly timber. It is now occupied by Vestas, who supports the offshore wind farm of thirty turbines owned by Vattenfall. (Canterbury District Council)

Union Transport Group's ships *Union Pluto* and *Union Neptune* bring regular cargoes of stone to Bretts tarmac plant at Whitstable. (A.L.)

Pleasure steamers occasionally make calls at Whitstable but it is very unusual to see two berthed together. The *Kingswear Castle* has arrived from Strood in October 2001 on a round trip and the *Waverley* is inward bound into the Thames en route for Tower Pier. (A.L.)

5

MARGATE

For Margate.

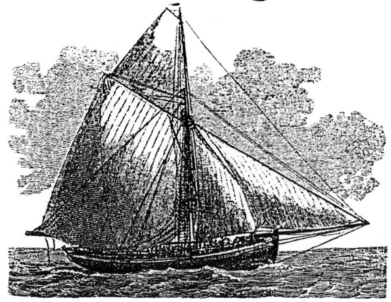

The BRITANNIA Yacht,

JOHN FINCH,

JAMES GORE, Master,

SAILS from DICE KEY for MARGATE every TUESDAY; and returns from thence for LONDON every FRIDAY during the Seafon. 1793.

The above YACHT is quite new, juft launched from DOVER, and is elegantly fitted up with every Accommodation for the Reception of Paffengers.

The Best Cabin Six Shillings.—Middle Cabin Four Shillings each.

The utmoft Care is taken of Baggage, Parcels, &c.

Jewels and Money will not be accounted for, unlefs paid for as fuch.

The MASTER to be fpoke with on BOARD, or at the IPSWICH ARMS, THAMES STREET.

Until the era of steam propulsion sailing hoys were the only means of travel by sea from London to Margate. Designed originally for the carriage of grain and other produce, they initially had only limited passenger capacity. This poster advertises the *Britannia*, built at Dover in 1793, which appears similar to the cutters used for the cross-Channel service. (Margate Museum)

In rough weather passages aboard the hoys could be long and uncomfortable. This cartoon entitled 'The Margate Hoy' published in January 1795 would not have encouraged travellers to use this form of transport. (Margate Museum)

'**THE PASSAGE PACKET** – Or yachts, as they are now called, are fitted with different cabins and beds, in a manner every way suitable for the reception of genteel passengers. During the season they sail every day, about an hour before high water, to and from Dice and Ralph's-quay, Billingsgate. The number of people carried to and from Margate in these vessels has been averaged at a moderate calculation at twenty thousand. Till 1803 not more than eight or nine packets were employed, which were then increased to eleven. During the summer months the passage is often made in eight or nine hours. The best wind from London is W. and for London, S.E. Some of the vessels have a state room, or after-cabin, which a select party engage for five or six guineas. Common passengers used to pay from five to seven shillings per head, with their baggage proportionally cheap. An advance in the prices of the passage has lately been made in addition to the increased tolls. But beside the yachts, there are two regular corn hoys, viz. The *Isle of Thanet*, Latham Osborn, owner. *Governor*, Daniel Swinford, owner; which sail alternately from Chester and Ralph's quays, near the Custom-house, on Saturdays and carry goods and passengers. It may be justly added, that the accommodation afforded, and the attention of the masters and seamen that navigate these vessels, are the reasons that Margate still continues to stand so high in the list of watering places.' (A Picture of Margate, 1809)

For MARGATE,
The FRANCIS Yacht,

ROBERT GOATHAM, MASTER.

Is now completely fitted up for Paffengers and Baggage, and will fail from CHESTER QUAY, near the Cuftom Houfe, every Wednefday, and from MARGATE every Sunday during the Seafon.

Paffengers FOUR SHILLINGS Each.

In this YACHT a Family or Party may be accommodated with a commodious private Apartment.

Takes in Goods, Paffengers, and Baggage for Ramfgate & Kingfgate.

The Mafter to be fpoke with on Board, or at the Harp, in Harp Lane, or HENRY SIMS for him, at the above Place, Thames Street.

Jewellery, Plate, and Money will not be accounted for unlefs paid as fuch.

Another advertisement for a passage to Margate contemporary with that of the *Britannia*. Note the craft are now generally referred to as yachts. A number of the Margate hoys were built by Whites at Broadstairs including the *Princess of Wales*, 75 tons, completed in 1795.

A hoy with few passengers aboard is passed by a crowded pleasure steamer. Although ridiculed and derided at first, after 1815 the paddle steamers quickly gained favour as they provided a much more reliable service. (*Illustrated London News*)

A list of the yachts and hoys that sail between Margate and London during the season in 1792; with their days of sailing.

Robert and Jane, Capt. Kidd, sails from Margate on Monday and returns on Thursday following. This vessel has three different cabins. Passage 10s 6d, 6s or 4s.

Dispatch, Capt. Laming, sails from Margate on Thursday, and returns on Monday. Passage 4s.

Prince of Wales, Capt. Finch, sails on Friday, and returns on Wednesday. Passage 4s.

Francis, Capt. Goatham, sails on Sunday, and returns on Wednesday. Passage 4s.

Endeavour, Capt. Kennard, sails on Sunday and returns on Saturday. Passage 4s.

The Rose in June, Capt. Palmer, sails from Margate on Wednesday, and returns on Sunday. Passage 4s.

The above vessels sail to Dice Quay, and Billingsgate Dock, Lower Thames Street, London, where answers are given respecting the hours of sailing.

There are also three corn hoys, which sail alternately from Margate to Galley Quay, near the Custom House, on Saturday and carry goods and passengers: they are the *Margate*, Capt. Walter; the *Isle of Thanet*, Capt. Pound; and the *Endeavour*, Capt. Minter. (Hall's New Margate Guide 1792.)

By 1796 there had been significant changes. The vessels sailing were as follows:

Robert and Jane, Capt. Kidd, was still sailing as in 1792 but the passage charges were now 5s, 7s and the after cabin 10s 6d for each passenger.

Royal Charlotte, Capt. James Laming, sails from Margate on Monday, and returns on Friday. Passage 5s and 7s.

Britannia, Capt. Finch, sails on Friday and returns on Wednesday. Passage 5s and 7s.

Diligence, Capt. Sandwell, sails from Margate on Saturday and returns on Wednesday. Passage 5s and 7s.

Duke of York, Capt. Kennard, sails on Tuesday and returns on Saturday. Passage 5s and 7s.

The New Rose in June, Capt. Palmer, sails from Margate on Wednesday and returns on Sunday. Passage 5s, 7s and the after cabin 10s 6d.

Princess of Wales, Capt. Hillier, sails from Margate on Wednesday and returns on Sunday. Passage 5s 7s and the after cabin 10s 6d.

British Queen, Capt. R. Laming, sails from Margate on Thursday and returns on Monday. Passage 5s and 7s.

The London destination of Dice quay was the same as in 1792. The corn hoy *Margate* was now commanded by Capt. Goodburne, the *Endeavour* by Captain Watler, and the *Isle of Thanet* by Capt. Minter. These three were now sailing alternately to Chester's quay, near the Custom House.

The first steamship to Margate on 3 July 1815

A New Superior and Certain Passage from Margate to London in a Day.

'The *THAMES* STEAM YACHT will start from Margate every Monday, Wednesday and Friday at 8 o'clock in the morning and leave Wool Quay, Customs House, Thames Street to return to Margate on every Tuesday, Thursday and Saturday. Fares: First Cabin: 15s, Second Cabin 11s. Pier Duty included. Children under 12, half price. (Kentish Gazette, 30 June 1815.)

'She is rapid, spacious, and indeed a splendid vessel. Her cabins are large and are fitted up with all that elegance could suggest or that personal comfort could require. She presents a choice library, and backgammon, draught boards and other amusements are provided. For the express purpose of combining delicacy with comfort, a stewardess tends on the fair sex.' (*The Times*, 8 July 1815.)

'The *Thames* carried a very tall smokestack which did duty as a mast on which a large square sail was set when the wind was favourable. A long outside gallery on which the cabins opened gave the impression that she was larger than she actually was, and with her row of gunports she presented a formidable appearance. (F. Burtt, *Steamers of the Thames and Medway*, 1949.)

'The *Thames* was originally built for the passage between Glasgow and Greenock and was first called the *Duke of Argyll*. She had an engine of 14 H.P. and was built of oak and fir. She was 79 feet long and 22 feet broad. She cost £2,500 to build and went from Portsmouth to Margate, 150 miles, on one ton of coal. She carried a large square sail and the funnel acted as a foremast.' (Watts Steam, *Yacht Guide*, 1820.)

'We went to see the steamboat come in from London. It is worked by means of two wheels, resembling water-wheels, one of which is placed on each side of the vessel, and about a half sunk in the water. It comes from London and returns three times in each week. It generally performs the voyage in about twelve hours... It is surprising to see how most people are prejudiced against this packet. Some say that it cannot sail against the wind if it is high, but when it entered the harbour the wind and tide were both against it, and the former rather rough, yet I saw it stem both. There was a great crowd, and much enthusiasm, though carpers predicted failure, and sneered at "smoke-jacks".' (*The Life of Sir Rowland Hill and the History of Penny Postage*, 1880.)

The *Thames* only remained on this service for a year but many others soon followed, such as the *London Engineer* left of 315 tons. She was built in 1818 with machinery of an experimental design driving internal paddle wheels turning at 28rpm. At 120ft she was considerably longer than the *Thames* and could carry at least 270 passengers, but she too had a relatively short life on the Margate service.

Another paddle steamer built in 1818 was the *Victory* of 160 tons, seen here approaching the stone pier at Margate in company with another steamer. Unlike the *London Engineer* she had a long life on the Margate service, apparently colliding with a collier brig off Barking in 1842 when she had 400 passengers on board. She was fortunate not to sink.

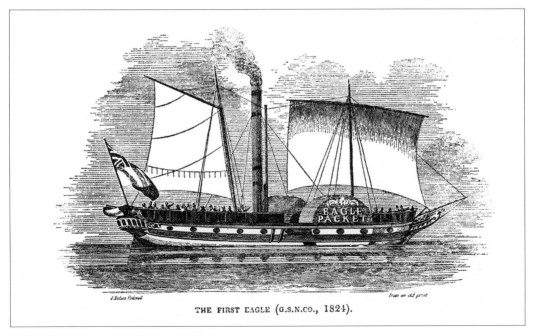

THE FIRST EAGLE (G.S.N.CO., 1824).

The General Steam Navigation Co., incorporated in 1824, eventually gained supremacy over all others. The wooden paddle steamer *Eagle* of 170 tons and built in 1820 on the Thames was acquired by the GSNC in 1824 and placed on the London–Thanet service. She was to be followed by a number of *Eagles* in later years.

Margate Pier – The stone pier seen below which encloses the harbour and supports the lighthouse was commenced in 1810, and finished in 1815. It was built under the direction of Sir John Rennie. Some contemporary accounts follow:

'It is constructed of Whitby stone, and its grey appearance presents a striking contrast to the white and yellow shades of the modern "box" breakwater. The arm is about 900 feet long, and the cost of building it was in the neighbourhood of £60,000.'

The Harbour Lighthouse – 'A beautiful and important stone building, it was completed in 1829, from the designs and under the superintendence of Mr. W. Edmunds, a native architect. The shaft forms an elegant Grecian Doric column, placed on an octagonal base, which serves as a watch house for sailors, and is surmounted by a richly ornamented chamber, or lantern, of cast iron.'

Jarvis's Landing Stage – 'This useful work was completed in 1824 at the cost of £8,000, which was, with extraordinary liberality, entirely born by the company of pier proprietors from whom it must therefore be regarded as a munificent gift to the public. It is constructed of English oak, measures 1,120 feet in length and, at low and half-tide, is deservedly considered one of the most inviting marine walks which fancy can imagine or experience realise.'

'It had the disadvantage of being completely submerged at high water. Until the present jetty was opened, excursion steamers used the harbour pier when they arrived during high water, and the old oak landing stage when the tide was out.'

The Iron Jetty – Replaced Jarvis's Landing Stage. The first section of the jetty was completed in 1853. It was afterwards lengthened, and, apart from harbour breakwaters, was the second longest pier on the mainland of Kent. It was damaged by fire and rough weather on several occasions, collapsing finally in the storm of February 1978. The stone pier lighthouse fell during the earlier storm of 31 January 1953, which caused widespread flooding on the east coast.

This view of the entrance to the iron jetty at Margate, taken probably from the Metropole Hotel, shows the popularity of the steamers in the Edwardian period. Posters offer trips by the Belle Steamers, General Steam Navigation vessels and New Palace steamers. The only building recognisable today is the Droit House, on the left, but even that has been replaced as the original was destroyed during the Second World War.

The *Koh-I-Noor* was a popular steamer of this period. She was built by Fairfields at Govan in 1892 at a cost of £50,000 and was at that time the largest and fastest steamer on the Thames. Initially she ran from Old Swan Pier to Southend and Clacton but was soon moved to the Thanet service, becoming for some years the Saturday 'Husbands' Boat' and making two trips daily from Tilbury to Margate. She survived until the end of the First World War.

THE NEW PALACE STEAMERS, LTD.
DAILY SEA TRIPS from MARGATE.

"LA MARGUERITE,"

Tonnage 2,204. Horse Power 7,500. Speed 20 Knots.

Mondays and Wednesdays to

OSTEND & BACK,

At 9.45 a.m., for LONDON 6.30 p.m.

Tuesdays to

BOULOGNE & BACK,

At 10 a.m., and for LONDON at 6 p.m.

Thursdays to

CALAIS & BACK,

At 11.30 a.m., for LONDON 6 p.m.

SATURDAYS for SOUTHEND & LONDON at 2 p.m.

SUNDAYS, 2 HOURS' SEA TRIP at 3 p.m. Fare 1/6.
Leaves for LONDON at 5.15 p.m.

Fares · Boulogne or Calais, 1st Saloon Return 7/6 ; 2nd Saloon Return 6/6.
　　　　Ostend　-　-　,, 　,,　,,　8/- ; 　,,　,,　,,　7/-.

"ROYAL SOVEREIGN,"
Daily to RAMSGATE at 2.15 p.m., and to LONDON 4 p.m.

"KOH-I-NOOR,"
DAILY (Tuesdays and Fridays excepted), at 3.15 p.m., for

SOUTHEND & LONDON (Saturdays 6.30 p.m. for Tilbury only)
The above Sailing Times subject to alterations during the Season.—See Handbills.

D. A. MACLACHLAN, Agent, The Jetty, Margate.
June 1903.　　　　　　　Telephone No. 107, Margate.

An even larger and more opulent steamer from Fairfield's was the *La Marguerite* of 1894. Capable of 20 knots, she was for ten years an immensely popular excursion steamer, running mainly on the Boulogne service. In spite of her following she did not make a profit and in 1904 was sold to Liverpool where she was a success, partly due to the much lower price of coal in the north. (Margate Museum)

Belle Steamers staff pose outside their booking office on Margate Jetty in 1905. (Margate Museum)

The largest of the *Belle* steamers, the *London Belle* approaches the jetty at Margate on a summer excursion. Requisitioned by the Admiralty in March 1916, she performed meritorious war service, at one time towing a German bombing airship which had come down in the estuary to Sheerness. She was sold to the Royal Sovereign Steam Ship Co. in 1924 and broken up in 1929.

This final representative from the golden era of steam travel on the Thames is the *Golden Eagle*. The General Steam Navigation had since 1824 built up a large fleet of paddle steamers, and this vessel continued their success. She was built by John Brown at Clydebank in 1909 and became very popular, making daily trips to Margate and Ramsgate with occasional visits to Boulogne. *Golden Eagle* served through two world wars and was eventually broken up in 1951.

Magnificent Saloon Steamer

"LONDON BELLE"

FIRST BOAT
EVERY MONDAY, TUESDAY, WEDNESDAY and THURSDAY

TO   RETURN
(Available day of issue only)

SOUTHEND 4/-

8 HOURS ASHORE INCLUDING FREE ADMISSION TO KURSAAL

MARGATE 6/-

4 HOURS ASHORE

Leaving   **GREENWICH PIER** -   -   -   -   **7.50 a.m.**
NORTH WOOLWICH PIER   -   -   **8.20 a.m.**
FIRST SAILING MONDAY, 20th JUNE

For **DAILY SERVICE** (Fridays excepted), see other Bills, or apply
GREENWICH: Pier Booking Boxes, or 29 London Street
WOOLWICH: Pier Booking Box, or 196 High Street, North East Ham.

HEAD OFFICE: R.S. Steamship Co. Ltd., 7, Swan Lane E.C.4   Telephone: CENTRAL 9220

H.B. BLAND & CO. (printers), 1, DUCKSFOOT LANE, LONDON, E.C.4

Running concurrently with *Koh-I-Noor* and *La Maguerite* was the *London Belle*, at 738 tons the largest of the Belle Steamers. She was built in 1893 by Denny's of Dumbarton, famous for their turbine steamers. This poster dates from 1927, close to the end of her service. (Margate Museum)

A view of Margate Jetty taken from near the Winter Gardens between the wars. The three steamers moored alongside indicate that the popularity of the resort has not diminished. (A.H. & S. Paragon Series)

Once the excursion vessels returned to service in 1946, the paddle steamers were gradually phased out and the new Denny motor ships *Royal Sovereign* (1948) and *Queen of the Channel* (1950) joined their twin-funnelled predecessor, the *Royal Daffodil* of 1939, shown here providing a regular summer service until its closure in 1966. Sadly the *Royal Daffodil* was broken up at Ghent in 1967. So ended a service which had existed since 1815. (A. Duncan)

6

RAMSGATE

This engraving by Storer from an original sketch by a Mr Orme of the eastern end of the harbour dates from 1795. It shows the storehouse demolished by Wyatt in 1803 and the tower of the old Committee House beyond. The dry dock and sluices for clearing the outer harbour of silt appear in the foreground. (Ramsgate Maritime Museum)

FOR

Ramsgate, Broadstairs,
AND ALL PLACES ADJACENT,
At BOTOLPH WHARF,
NEAR LONDON BRIDGE,

The following Vessels will sail in the Summer Season:
RESOLUTION, *James Kelsey, on Sunday,*
SWIFT, *Edward Harman, on Wednesday,*
LORD HAWKESBURY, *George Ansell, on Friday,*

(AND ONCE A WEEK DURING WINTER.)
TAKES IN PASSENGERS AND GOODS FOR THE FOLLOWING PLACES,

RAMSGATE	**ST. PETERS**	**PEGWELL**	**MINSTER**
BROADSTAIRS	**ST. LAWRENCE**	**MONKTON**	**MANSTONE**

And all Places adjacent

BEST CABIN, 7s.—FORE CABIN, 5s.—each Passenger.—Children in Arms, Half Price.

N. B. No Vessels at any other Wharf.

The Master or Wharfinger for him, to be spoken with on Board, at the Newcastle Coffee House, St Mary Hill, at the Gun Tavern, Billingsgate, or S. WILLIAMS, on the Irish Walk in 'Change Hours, for them.
You are requested to send the Wharfage with your Goods, and a Sufferance, or apply at the 'Counting House for the same.
Not accountable for Loss by Fire, or the Dangers and Accidents of the Sea and Navigation.

Received   *Wharfage*
           Sufferance

Cooke, Printer, Dunstan's Hill.

A poster advertising hoys making passages to Ramsgate from London around the same period as the engraving above. Passengers would usually get off at Margate to travel overland, thus avoiding the sometimes turbulent North Foreland. Only their baggage was brought to Ramsgate by sea. (Tom White)

This painting by K.B. Martin (Harbourmaster, 1836–1859) shows the western end of the harbour as it would have appeared in the first half of the eighteenth century. It includes the King's Head, which as the major building to the right is the site occupied by the later Royal Hotel. Military Road was later built under the cliffs to the left. (Ramsgate Maritime Museum)

An atmospheric engraving based on a drawing by E.W. Cooke showing various craft entering Ramsgate Harbour in rough weather, including a cutter-rigged smack. Samuel Wyatt's lighthouse on the west pier was completed in 1795. The present one, built by John Shaw, replaced it in 1842. (Geo. Virtue)

An engraving showing the west cliff about 100 years later than the subject of K.B. Martin's painting. The Georgian houses are largely complete and the base of Military Road is also visible beneath the cliffs. The latter was built to supply ships at the time of the Napoleonic Wars. (Dugdales)

A view along Harbour Parade from about 1890. Sailing colliers are moored alongside the Town Quay and a variety of horse-drawn carts carry merchandise along the street. The Royal Hotel has been replaced but the buildings on the right are still in existence, with the exception of the Albion Hotel which was demolished in 1893.

A view looking eastwards along Military Road in the direction of the Admiral Harvey Inn which is believed to date from around 1850. The three store houses with gabled roofs just visible at extreme right appear the same as those in the picture at upper left on the previous page.

This impressive view across the harbour shows a variety of wherries, fishing smacks and larger sailing vessels in the inner basin at a similar time to the view along Harbour Parade opposite. The Albion Hotel was replaced by the National Provincial Bank in 1898. The building remained a bank until 1998 when it became Pizza Express. (Tom White)

Two of the crew pose for a photograph on a ship moored to the cross-wall at Ramsgate. In late Victorian days the port was very busy, often crowded with fishing smacks, the quays lined with collier brigs and barquentines. Disabled vessels also sought refuge here in stormy weather.

A general view of the inner basin of Ramsgate Harbour with the typical vessels unloading at the quays and the smacks moored out in the centre in a rather random distribution. This postcard allows a direct comparison with the view below. The smacks became almost as abundant, reaching a peak of close to 170 in the Edwardian period. (British Mirror Series)

Leisure craft have taken over from the smacks in this photograph taken in 2009. The marina at Ramsgate now has some 700 berths in the inner and outer sections of the old Royal Harbour. The one unchanged feature is the slipway, which seems to have regular work whatever the decade. (A.L.)

A view across the harbour from the cross-wall on a quiet day. This illustration shows clearly the stern of the fishing smack *Prudence*. The fact that the National Provincial Bank has now replaced the Albion Hotel suggests the date might be around 1903. Yachts have by now replaced the collier brigs on the Town Quay.

A picture taken from almost the same position and at almost the same time as the one above shows a sailing ship alongside unloading cargo into horse-drawn carts, the normal means of transport for the period. (Arthur D. Lewis, *The Kent Coast*)

In the last years of the nineteenth century, Smeaton's dry dock at the eastern end of the harbour was converted into an ice house by the Isle of Thanet Ice Co. The Ramsgate Smack-Owners Ice Co. already had an ice house at the end of Military Road, which is still in existence. Background features include buoys belonging to the Trinity House Depot, a warehouse at centre and the Trustees Meeting House at right. (Tom White)

Ice shipments arrived regularly from Norway. Most were used by the fishing fleet to preserve their catches but some was bought by the railway company, similarly to preserve fish in transit to the London markets. Many smacks unloaded their fish near Billingsgate in London directly, to avoid delays. (Tom White)

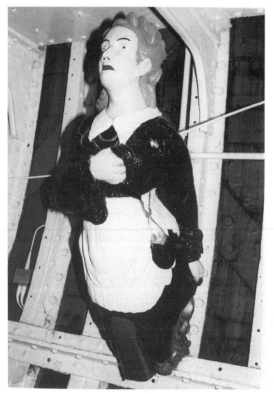

Above: The barquentine *Old Goodey* was originally built as a schooner at Sandwich in 1865. She had Whitstable owners and was a regular trader to Ramsgate, colliding with one of the piers in August 1889. Dismasted in 1910 she was converted to a hulk. Her figurehead was purchased by a Faversham butcher who fixed it above his shop. (Tom White)

Left: The *Old Goodey*'s figurehead was later purchased by Mr Sidney Silver Cumbers and, after restoration, placed in his 'Long John Silver' collection aboard the *Cutty Sark*. (A.L.)

Ramsgate's shipbuilders were initially situated to the east of the harbour but when the London Chatham & Dover Railway proposed building a station on the sands they were faced with relocation. The yards of Miller & Co., Strong Barnes & Co., and of Samuel Beeching and Thomas Moses were cleared. Land was made available to the west of the harbour where only Beeching and Moses set up the yard seen here. (Raphael Tuck)

Last of the fishing smacks to be built by the firm of Beeching and Moses at Ramsgate was the *Clipper* (R.237) in 1913. This model forms part of the collection of the Ramsgate Maritime Museum. It was later carefully restored by model-maker Geoff Michell, who kindly provided this photograph.

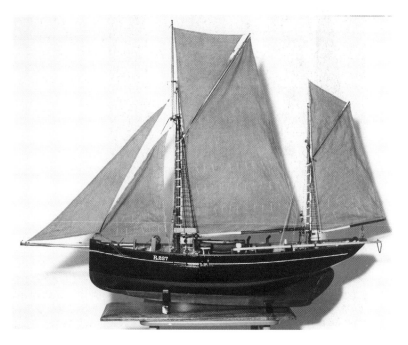

Ramsgate Steam Drifters and Trawlers

Name	Number	Place of Build	Registered	Fate
Acceptable	R 78 (Dr.)	1911 Yarmouth	1919	Sold to Lowestoft in 1924
Boy Nat	R 116	Selby	1920	Sold to Lowestoft in 1930
Caister Castle	R 120 (Tr.)	1914 Yarmouth	1920	Lost by stranding at Linney Head in 1921
Campanula	R 105 (Dr.)	1913 Yarmouth	1919	Lost with all hands January 1920
Charde (ex-*Hurricane*)	R 90 (Dr.)	1919 Lowestoft	1919	Sunk in collision on Government service 21.6.40
Constance Mary	R 372			
Excel	R 373 (Dr.)	1907 Aberdeen	1922	Sold to Lowestoft in 1929
Explorator	R 15 (Dr.)	1909 Lowestoft	1925	Broken up at Ramsgate 1929
Feasible	R 157 (Dr.)	1912 Aberdeen	1920	Sold to Lowestoft in 1930
Garrigill	R 267 (Dr.)	1914 Yarmouth	1920	Lost with all hands Aug. 1934
George Hay	R 51 (Dr.)	1912 Portgordon	1927	Sold to Lowestoft in 1929
Glentilt	(Dr.)	1900	1920	Later *Glenealy*
Gust	R 347 (Dr.)	1918 Aberdeen	1920	Sold to Peterhead in 1922
Harvest Moon	R 148 (Dr.)	1904 Yarmouth	1920	Sold as blockship for R. Stour 9.9.40
Kentish Belle (ex-*Tiderip*)	R 94 (Dr.)	1919 Lowestoft	1919	Sunk in collision Feb. 1923
Kestrel	R 7	Yarmouth	1929	Lost by enemy action 28.3.41
Lady Luck	R 355	Montrose	1921	Sold to Milford Haven. Broken up in 1956
Loyal Star	R 246 (Dr.)	1913 Yarmouth	1920	Sold Milford Haven. Broken up in Nov. 1953
Mary Evelyn	R 333	Lowestoft	1920	Sunk in collision in June 1932
Mill o'Buckie	R 129 (Dr.)	1914 Aberdeen	1920	Sold to Milford Haven. Broken up in Dec. 1957
Murk	R 345 (Dr.)	1918 Aberdeen	1920	Sold to Lowestoft in 1922
Ocean Pride	R 243 (Dr.)	1911 Middlesborough	1920	Sold to Inverness in 1925
Olivae	R 212 (Dr.)	1915 Yarmouth	1920	Sold to Lowestoft in 1924
Paramount	R 193 (Dr.)	1911 Selby	1920	Sold Milford Haven. Broken up in 1955
Provider	R 19 (Dr.)	1907 Appledore	1930	Sold 1949. Broken up in 1954
Queen	R 143	Aberdeen	1920	Sold to Buckie in 1926
Resplendent	R 192 (Dr.)	1914 Aberdeen	1920	Sold to Milford Haven. Broken up in July 1954
Rig	R 139 (Dr.)	1911 Alloa	1920	Sold to Milford Haven. Broken up December 1957
Spectrum	R 343 (Dr.)	1918 Lowestoft	1920	Sold to Wick in 1922
Sunshine	R 172 (Tr.)	1900 Lowestoft	1920	Registry transferred to Colchester in 1929
Tankerton Towers (ex-*Setweather*)	R 96 (Dr.)	1918 Lowestoft	1919	Lost by enemy action 9.5.41
Treasure	R 37 (Dr.)	1907 Aberdeen	1931	Broken up in May 1949
Tweenways	R 356 (Dr.)	1920 Montrose	1921	Sold to Danish Owners in 1947
Uberty	R 219 (Dr.)	1912 Aberdeen	1920	Sold to Milford Haven in 1932
Unicity (ex-*Bubble*)	R 22 (Dr.)	1919 Lowestoft	1926	Owned at Milford Haven when lost on Government service in Jan. 1942
Wishful	R 159 (Dr.)	1910 Selby	1919	Sunk in collision in 1921

In spite of the ability to release water from the inner harbour rapidly through sluices, Ramsgate's outer harbour has always suffered from silting, and has thus required frequent dredging. The bucket-dredger *Hope*, left, was built by Fleming & Ferguson at Paisley in 1901 and served until 1936. She discharged the silt into barges which were moored alongside. These were towed to sea by the harbour tug *Aid* for dumping.

The *Hope* was replaced in 1936 by the *Ramsgate*, which kept the port clear until 1962. A second vessel of that name was built by W.J. Yarwood & Sons at Northwich, Cheshire, in 1962. Both were grab-dredgers with hoppers. After forty-five years of service the later *Ramsgate*, seen here, was sold to Fleetwood in December 2007. The use of the sluices in the inner harbour was abandoned in March 1985 owing to the adverse effect on the marina berths. (A.L.)

A harbour regatta was held at Ramsgate in August of every year prior to the First World War. Swimming events were very popular.

In the late 1880s the London-based Temple Yacht Club set up a further headquarters in Ramsgate, and on 30 May 1896 moved into their present premises. Yachts afterwards replaced the colliers alongside the Town Quay and this Admiralty steam yacht may have attended the club's opening in 1896 or the time when the title 'Royal' was conferred on it a year or so later. (Tom White)

For those who did not have their own boats there was the possibility of a trip to sea on a passenger yacht. Here the *Prince Frederick William* leaves harbour under full sail. This 24-ton cutter was the last vessel built by Caught's at Ramsgate in 1858. She had a long life, returning to fishing in her latter days.

Another popular vessel was the 64ft *Moss Rose*, seen here leaving the Dover Steps on the east pier under tow, probably by the harbour tug. She was built by Joseph Legg at Penzance in 1878. Her rig is reminiscent of the earlier hoys. In calm conditions these cutters needed assistance to clear the harbour entrance. (Tom White)

The Ramsgit Boat

'The selection of the right boat for the right place was very much a matter of luck. "This way for Margit an' 'Ern Bay! Hinside boat for Margit!" "Ramsgate boat?" "No, mum; that's 'er, blowin' hoff steam and ringin' 'er bell; the houtside boat for Ramsgit, over the Margit and Gravesend boats. Don't you mind what nobody says, but just keep arter me mum." And so, closely following an active little man with a big porter's knot, upon which he had balanced half a truck-load of baggage, the expedition picks its way in single file along the narrow crowded pavement, down steep steps, and out among slimy piles, round which a hollow sound reverberates from the swell of the water as it moves to and fro between them. At last a sense of real repose and safety follows that perilous struggle from Billingsgate to the deck of the Ramsgate boat... Like most other steamboats about to sail for distant parts, the *Duchess of Kent*, with a roar of steam and a ringing of bells, is doing her best to confuse the head and ear of the leader of the expedition, as he tries to count his baggage and eliminate the "regular charges" from the extortionate claims of a dozen ruffians, who having captured his boxes on shore, now turn up in a surprising manner with them on board the boat.

'Landing at Ramsgate in those days was very peaceful, with helping hands ready to assist each member of the expedition on shore. For year after year the same family would rent the same little furnished house or cottage; so that it came to pass that quite friendly relations sprang up between the proprietors of such houses, and the members of these annual outings. The little "Marine Views" and "Cliff Cottages," with their black flint facings and green outer shutters, were usually the property of some retired pilot or provident master of a lugger; and were very unlike the rows of four-storied tenements let now in first, second and third floors. The rooms were small but there was an individuality about them, and the furniture was such as is never found in the seaside lodging of today. Old sea-fights and scripture prints hung thickly round the walls; while one seldom missed a pair of rude portraits of the landlord and his "missus," "took when they were younger than they be now."... And so, surrounded by old friends, the expedition finds itself seated once more at the well-known little tea-table, with good home-made bread, fresh butter, plenty of milk and cream, and a quart of large brown Pegwell Bay shrimps as a particular relish.' (Leslie, Robert C., *A Sea-Painter's Log*, 1886)

It was important not to forget the refreshments. (Bamforth & Co.)

A Voyage to Ramsgate

'The Nore [lightship] was considered a sort of half-way house between London and Ramsgate, and was looked upon with interest by the younger members of the expedition as having been the model upon the lines of which they considered their favourite toy Noah's Ark was built; besides, after passing it, they were invited by the steward to dinner in the saloon. And what dinners they were - what ribs of roast beef, what splendid potatoes smoking in their jackets! How trident like were the big three-pronged steel forks, with strange green horn handles and round-ended knife blades to match them. And was there ever such ginger beer and bottled stout, such big apple-tarts, such custard pudding? After dinner there was the breezy deck again, with Herne Bay Pier in sight, and its little schooner-rigged tram sailing down it, to meet the boat, if the wind allowed. While on board the old *Duchess* herself we had canvas set fore and aft - not mere scraps of sails to steady the boat or help the draught of her engine fires, but honest old-fashioned mainsail, foresail, and staysail, straining at their sheets, and pulling the old ship nearly a knot faster through the water than she could have gone without them. There were no bridges in those days; and the ship was steered aft by the mysterious "man at the wheel," never to be spoken to on any pretext. Among the passengers, however, were always one or two privileged people who had often rounded the Foreland in tremendous weather, who knew the captain, and all the landmarks nearly as well as he did himself. These men smoked strong cigars up even to the awful moment when, after rolling and pitching for an hour or more from the Margate Roads to the Foreland, we tumbled and plunged between the piers into Ramsgate Harbour itself. And they *would* speak to the man at the wheel; while less nautical passengers hung upon their words as upon those of an oracle.' (Leslie, Robert C., *A Sea-Painter's Log*, 1886)

In late Victorian times London families would often spend a few weeks on the coast in summertime. The husbands still had to work, however, and had only the weekends to see their wives and children. They came down by the so-called 'Husband's Boat' on Saturdays and returned on Sundays. This comic postcard gives some indication of the clamour on the boat's arrival at Ramsgate. (Valentine's series)

The steamboats were as popular at Ramsgate as they were at Margate. Here the *Royal Sovereign* calls at the end of the east pier. She was a very popular steamer on the route, running between 1893 and 1929.

After the holiday it was time to return to London. This close-up view shows passengers boarding the *Royal Sovereign*, some with trunks and others with large cases. (Frederick E. Phillpott)

The Royal Victoria Pavilion was built close to the eastern side of the harbour on land previously occupied by the shipbuilders and later by stonemasons working on repairs and additions to the harbour. It was opened in 1904 by Princess Louise, daughter of Queen Victoria. This view shows the pavilion shortly after its completion.

This statue, now missing a hand, still decorates the original entrance of the Victoria Pavilion but virtually all of the rest of the decorative detail has been lost. Very active in its day, a fully licensed roof garden and sun deck was created on the first storey. Seaside shows were presented and later a hall of mirrors was installed at the upper level. In recent years the building was converted into a casino and now lies empty in a sad state, awaiting redevelopment. (A.L.)

Another building of interest on the harbour is the Clock House, dating from 1817. Initially the western end was occupied by Trinity House and used for buoy maintenance, and the large door opening they needed still remains. Trinity House left in 1914, as did the General Steam Navigation who occupied the foyer. The Forelands and Globe fishing companies resided there in the twenties. It is at present home to the Ramsgate Maritime Museum.

At the western end of the harbour lie the Sailors Church (left) and the Smack Boy's Home. The former dates from 1878 and the latter 1881. Both were the result of the Revd Eustace Brennan's concern for the spiritual and physical welfare of the apprentices employed on the fishing smacks and other seafarers. (A.L.)

Ramsgate became famous at the time of the retreat from Dunkirk when some 82,000 men were brought to the port in every kind of craft imaginable. Some idea of the vessels involved can be gained from this photograph.

The *New Britannic*, shown here some years ago at Ramsgate, was a successor to the *Moss Rose* and *Prince Frederick William* and now belongs to the Dunkirk Little Ships Restoration Trust. She is a 56ft passenger launch dating from 1930 and is credited with lifting some 3,000 men from the beaches and carrying them out to waiting ships. (A.L.)

A slipway has formed part of the harbour facilities since 1835. The harbour authority, be it the Board of Trade, or at present the Thanet District Council, have leased it to various operators over the years who have always been busy. In this early view a Trinity House light tender is having its bow repaired. (Harold Holladay)

A three-masted barque on the slipway in about 1880. (Ramsgate Maritime Museum)

Claxton & Co., who leased the Ramsgate slipway for trawler maintenance, were absorbed by London tug-owners William Watkins in 1921. After that date all of Watkins' tugs were refitted at Ramsgate, a long association with the London River that ended when the *Kenia*, shown here, left the port on 17 January 1961. (*East Kent Times*).

Although the Trinity House Depot at Ramsgate closed in 1914, their craft are occasionally brought to the port for refitting. Here automatic light vessel No.24 is being repainted in November 2000. The draught of these vessels means they can only be launched on the top of spring tides. (A.L.)

In the post-war years, trade reached a peak with the London dock strike of 1955 when many vessels came to Ramsgate with perishable cargoes. Unfortunately the visits were not maintained due to a shortage of warehousing space. In this view, from around 1960, the *Reginald Kearon* has brought in a cargo of timber to the west quay. (A.L.)

An early aggregate dredger, the *Sand Grebe*, leaves the cross-wall at Ramsgate in early 1962. Sea-dredged aggregates have grown greatly in quantity and importance in more recent times. (A.L.)

One trade that came to Ramsgate due to a ship's diversion during the dock strike was the importation of Volkswagen motor cars from Emden. Ships were calling regularly by 1959. This view shows a Coles mobile crane unloading a VW Beetle from the MV *Butjadingen* around 1962. Muller's vessels *Aphaia*, *Alexis* and *Agenor* were usually used for these shipments. (A.L.)

After the commercial quay was completed in 1973 in the outer harbour at Ramsgate, larger ships were able to call. Specialised car carriers with a stern-loading arrangement were then used. United European Car Carriers (UECC) held the contract for Volkswagen-Audi car shipments in the latter days before the work was moved to Sheerness in 1994. (A.L.)

Ramsgate still has a very active fishing industry with some twenty-five boats of under 10m working from the port. Three boats fish for whelks as well as white fish and two combine lobsters with traditional fishing. Sole, plaice and skate are the white fish mainly caught, some 260 tons being landed in 2008. (A.L.)

The RNLI has maintained a lifeboat at Ramsgate for many years and the station has many famous rescues to its credit and must stand high in the medal league table. The *Esme Anderson* is seen here berthed at the end of the commercial jetty beneath the impressive boat house. Such accommodation is relatively new, the crew having had to suffice with sharing part of the Clock House for many years. (A.L.)

The extension of the harbour westwards during the 1980s allowed ferry services to begin with France and later Belgium. The main operator was Sally Line, working to Dunkirk. In 1994, however, the Belgian State Railways (RMT) ferries moved from Dover to Ramsgate, bringing the *Prins Filip*, at 28,000 gross tons, the largest vessel ever to enter the port. She did not stay for long because the Belgian railways withdrew from owning ferries in February 1998 and their ships were sold. They did not all leave, however, because the current *Eurovoyager* running for TransEuropa Ferries was originally RMT's *Prince Albert*. (A.L.)

The day following the last Belgian ferry sailing to Ostende on 28 February 1997, Holyman Sally Ferries started operating on the same route with two catamarans, the *Holyman Rapide* and *Holyman Diamant*. This was also unfortunately a short-lived service and in November 1998 Sally Line also halted their Dunkirk service. The two catamarans were sold to Hoverspeed, who continued the Ostende service from Dover, retaining the names *Rapide* and *Diamant*. (A.L.)

The *Eurotraveller* (earlier named the *Sally Sky*) sails for the last time to Dunkirk from Ramsgate under Sally colours in November 1998. She later returned as the *Larkspur* of TransEuropa Ferries (A.L.)

Almost immediately TransEuropa Ferries commenced a service to Ostende with the *Primrose* (another ex-Belgian ferry) and *Eurovoyager*. The *Laburnum* was acquired shortly afterwards as well as the *Larkspur*. The *Gardenia*, here seen at Ramsgate in the spring of 2009, is a more recent addition. She was originally the *European Endeavour*. (A.L.)

The latest major development at Ramsgate is the construction of the Thanet offshore wind farm, comprising one hundred turbines. The barge *Sea Jack* belonging to A2SEA is seen on one of her first visits. *Sea Jack* is towed out to the wind farm site to place each of the immense monopiles in its correct position. Only two can be accommodated at a time. (A.L.)

Two of the wind farm monopiles which form the almost submerged base of each turbine are shown on their delivery barge moored alongside the east pier in June 2009. These monopiles are 60m in length and 4.1-4.5m in diameter. Each weighs around 500 tons. (A.L.)

Estuary Services Ltd have operated launches out of Ramsgate since 1988, placing Medway and Thames pilots on ships inward bound or landing them from vessels outward bound. They operate in almost all weathers and the 49ft Estuary-class of boats have done sterling service since their arrival in 1992. Capable of 25 knots, the *Estuary Warden* here approaches a vessel destined for the Medway. (A.L.)

This group aboard the pilot launch comprise two senior Port of London Authority pilots, Chris Renault at left rear and Philip Deschamps, with two trainees, Jean Buckpitt and Pankaj Raina. As may be imagined, the trip from ship to shore is not always comfortable. (A.L.)

7

DOVER

Left: Dover was a port of great significance in Roman times and as such two lighthouses were built on the heights on either side of the River Dour to mark the entrance. Only the Pharos in Dover Castle is recognisable today but it is believed that they both originally appeared as in this drawing.

Below: Due to silting, the harbour was moved after the Norman Conquest to the west of the town in the area of Archcliffe fort, where a new basin called 'Paradise' was created. The build-up of shingle was still a problem and Henry VIII, one of the champions of Dover, subscribed to some major sea defence works to protect the harbour. Known usually as the Mole Rocks, they did not solve the problem. (British Museum)

Henry VIII departed from Dover with great ceremony in 1520 to meet with Francis I on the Field of the Cloth of Gold. A later splendid arrival was that of Charles II on 25 May 1660 to reclaim the throne. Unfortunately, due to the shingle having once more blocked the harbour, he had to land on the beach. In spite of this recurring problem numerous members of foreign and British royal families travelled through the port in the centuries that followed.

A scene typical of many royal arrivals, this picture is believed to depict the arrival at Dover of Princess Mary of Modena for her marriage to James, Duke of York, in 1673.

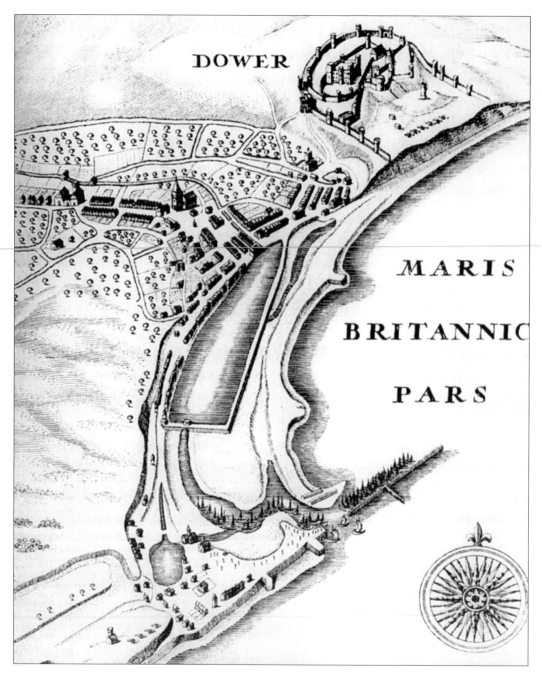

DOWER

MARIS

BRITANNIC

PARS

Various attempts were made to reduce the effects of the silting of the harbour. One of the most effective was made in 1583, when a reservoir fed by the River Dour called the Great Pent was constructed. Sluices could be opened which would release the water in a sudden rush through the entrance of the harbour. Seen in the centre of this drawing, it worked successfully for some years. The walls of the Great Pent, built by Sir Thomas Scott to the plans of Thomas Digges, involved works which for their date were almost on the scale of the later Admiralty Harbour. The Great Pent later became the Wellington Dock and Waterloo Crescent was built on the bank of shingle to seaward of it.

Some Ships Built at Dover

Name	Type of vessel	Tonnage (Builder's Measure -ment)	No. of guns	Dimensions (ft)	Builder	Date Built	Fate of Vessel
Ariel	6th rate	594	28	120.5 x 33.5	–	1785	Fate unknown
Belette	Brig-sloop 'Cruizer'-class	384	18		King	21.3.1806	Wrecked 24.11.1812 in the Kattegat
Cockatrice	Cutter	181	14	70 x 26	King	3.7.1781	Sold 9.1802
Drake	Brig-sloop	221	14	79 x 26	Ladd	5.1779	Condemned 7.1800 Jamaica
Echo	Sloop	341	16	96 x 29	King	9.1797	Sold 18.5.1809
Eclipse	Brig-sloop 'Cruizer'-class	384	18		King	4.8.1807	Sold 31.8.1817
Espoir	Brig-sloop 'Cruizer'-class	385	18		King	22.9.1804	Broken up 4.1821
Flirt	Brig-sloop	209	14	78 x 26	King	4.3.1782	Sold 1.12.1795
Harpy	Brig-sloop	316	18	95 x 28	King	2.1796	Sold 10.11.1817
Incendiary	Fireship	422	16	109 x 30	King	12.8.1782	Captured by French 29.1.1801 in Mediterranean
Lapwing	6th rate	598	28	120.5 x 34	King	21.9.1785	Broken up 5.1828
Leveret	Brig-sloop 'Cruizer'-class	384	18		King	14.1.1806	Wrecked 10.11.1807 on Galloper Rock
Speedy	Brig-sloop	208	14	78 x 26	King	29.6.1782	Captured 3.7.1801 by the French in Mediterranean (French 6.1794 to 3.95)
Sprightly	Cutter		10		King	16.8.1777	Capsized 12.1777 off Guernsey
Sprightly	Cutter	151	10	66 x 24	King	4.8.1778	Captured 10.2.1801 by the French in the Mediterranean and scuttled
Surly	Cutter	137	10	63 x 23.5	Johnson	15.11.1806	Sold 1.1837
Swallow	Sloop	226	14	79.5 x 26.5	Ladd	2.4.1779	Driven ashore 26.8.1781 near Long Island by four American privateers

Table source: J.J. Colledge, *Ships of the Royal Navy – An Historical Index.*

An aquatint showing a cutter entering Dover Harbour in 1819. A pilot manual for the period states that the best time to enter was about 1½ hours before high water. 'On the western pier head are two flag staffs; on the largest of which a red flag is kept up by day and a red light on each at night, while there is more than 10ft of water in the entrance.' (R. Havell and H. Whitfield)

The harbour was surveyed by John Scott Tucker in 1833. The Great Pent is still recognisable, while the earlier Paradise Pent has been filled in to build part of the Pier District. The rest of the harbour has been separated into an inner basin with an entrance lock (later the Granville Dock) and an outer tidal basin.

The Firſt HOY for DOVER

THE
Phœnix,
JOHN SUTTON,
THOMAS CHESTER and CO. Owners,
Takes in Goods and Paſſengers for

Dover . . .	Hythe	Romney . . .	Barham
Folkſtone . .	Dymchurch .	Lydd	Elham

And all Places adjacent,

Lying at BREWER's and CHESTER's Quay, Custom-House.

The Maſter to be spoken with on Board, at the Cooper's Arms, and at the Yorkshire Grey Thames Street; or the Wharfinger or John Tripeſs for him.

SATURDAY is the laſt Day of taking in.—A Veſſel sails from the above Quay every Week. No Goods taken in after Six o'Clock at Night.

The Owners or Master of the Veſſel will not be anſwerable for Damage or Loſs ariſing from any of the Dangers or Accidents of the Sea and of Navigation, of whatever Nature or Kind soever, to any Goods to be shipped on Board this Veſſel.—Not anſwerable for Loſs by Fire.

Advertising material was printed for hoys calling at Dover in the same manner as for the other Kent ports in the late eighteenth and early nineteenth centuries. This is a computer-generated reproduction of a damaged original.

& Hull.—Vessels for Colchester, Ipswich, Aldborough, Wisbeach, Dover, Yarmouth, Norwich,

From WOOL QUAY,
A Vessel every WEDNESDAY and SATURDAY,
FOR
DOVER,
Barham, Dymchurch, Eythorne, Hythe, Folkestone, Lydd, Romney, St. Margate,
AND ALL PLACES ADJACENT.
THE LORD FOLKESTONE PACKET,
William Salmon, Master.

Clears on

The Master to be spoken with on board, or Wharfinger for him on the the Quay.

You are particularly requested to send the Money for Wharfage & Sufferance with your Goods & describe their contents.

N.B. *The Wharfingers and Owners are not accountable for Loss by Fire, the Dangers and Accidents of the Sea and Navigation; or for any Goods not marked with the Name and Place of abode in full length; nor for Plate or Jewellery, unless paid for accordingly.*

Please not to advise your Correspondents till your Goods are on Board, as we will not be answerable for their going in this or any particular Vessel till they are actually shipped.

₊ The Wharfingers and Owners hereby give Notice, that they will not pay any claim for Loss or Damage, unless Application is made within Three Months from the Date of this Receipt.

No. of Packages.		s.	d.	Received by	184
	Wharfage &c,				
	Sufferance				

W. J. HALL, & Co. Wharfingers.
Warehouse Keepers, and Ship Brokers.

[Left margin:] Steam Vessels for Boulogne, Calais, Ostend, Antwerp, Rotterdam, Hambro'

[Right margin:] Gainsbro', Sunderland, Hartlepool, Margate, Boston, Lincoln, Woodbridge,

Canterbury & Whitstable, Deal & Sandwich, Blakeney & Wells, Harwich & Manningtree.

McKewan, Printer, 9, Great Winchester-street, Old Broad-street.

A similar bill advertises the steamer *Lord Folkestone*'s schedule for the 1840s.

Crossing the English Channel in the Early Nineteenth Century:

Accounts vary, but it was often not a pleasant experience for a variety of reasons:

'Nobody who has not personally experienced it can imagine the intolerable nuisances of the Channel crossing in the thirties. It was about 1828 or 1829 that I first travelled from London to Paris. The boat was met at Dover by a shoal of Custom House officers, who waylaid the wet, weary and frequently seasick passengers. Examination in those days was carried to the length of bodily search. You were felt all over to see whether you had anything concealed on your person. Ladies were taken into a separate room and underwent the same examination at the hands of a female attendant. This operation at Dover or Calais lasted from half-an-hour to one hour and a half, according to the number of passengers. The crossing frequently lasted eight hours. On landing, passports were severely scrutinized, to see whether they agreed with the description of the bearer, and if there was the slightest error, you were not allowed to proceed on the journey.' (Blount, Sir Edward, *Memoirs*)

1840: In three hours and a quarter from our starting, we found ourselves anchored in Dover Harbour, for unfortunately the tide would not serve for our getting into the pier. We therefore had no choice but landing by boat, and then commenced a system of Extortion, to which that on the opposite side would not compare. It was hoped 'that we would not object to pay four shillings each for landing us'. Vain hope! for I did object most decidedly doing anything of the kind, with a hint at the same time of leaving it to the Mayor to decide the point. This brought them down to the permitted charge of 2/6, accompanied by a hope that I would give them something for the luggage. That was declined – the boat grazed on the shingle, a board was placed, over which we walked, for which the modest demand of one shilling was made and satisfied. (Robert Goodsall, *A Fourth Kentish Patchwork*, 1974)

Lord Beaconsfield recounts in September 1839 making a rough but very rapid passage 'between Dover and Calais in only two hours and twenty minutes.' (Lord Beaconsfield's *Letters*, 1887)

When a cross-Channel sailing packet could not moor to the quay because of weather or tide the passengers were brought to the beach by small craft, known as 'faring' boats. This eighteenth-century print shows passengers being 'helped' ashore. The extortionate charging referred to above was eventually reduced by regulated porterage rates.

THE LORD WARDEN HOTEL, DOVER.

During the Victorian era the facilities at Dover improved markedly for travellers. One major advance for the more affluent was the building of the Lord Warden Hotel by the South Eastern Railway, near to the Admiralty Pier station in 1853. Amongst the many notable guests who stayed there was Charles Dickens. After the Second World War it was converted into offices and is currently occupied by the Dover Harbour Board.

An early grand occasion at the Lord Warden Hotel was the arrival of Napoleon III of France with Empress Eugenie on a six-day state visit on 16 April 1855. They were greeted at Dover by Prince Albert and a reception was held at the hotel as here recorded. Unfortunately he was later deposed and became a prisoner of the Prussians, eventually returning to Dover in 1871 as a refugee to be reunited with Eugenie at the same hotel.

HOTEL BURLINGTON, DOVER.

Another imposing hotel, the Clarence, was built in 1864 facing Clarence Lawn. In 1867 it was re-named the Imperial. Apparently far from successful, it was closed in 1871 and not re-opened until 1897, when it became the Burlington. The Promenade Pier was built to seaward from Clarence Lawn in 1893. After a period of success it was converted into flats in the 1930s but suffered severe damage in the last war. It was demolished in 1949.

Dover developed rapidly during the nineteenth century both as a resort and cross-Channel port. Marine Parade (1820) and Waterloo Crescent (1834) were built and bathing cabins became available as at Margate and Ramsgate. This photograph, taken from the Promenade Pier, dates from the end of the century. (Thornton Bros' *Balmoral* series)

Sailing craft were frequent callers at Dover. Leaving the port is the 207-ton barquentine *Waterwitch* of Fowey. She was built at Poole in 1871, originally as a brig, and was the last British square-rigged ship to trade under sail. A fast sailer in her time, she was sold to Estonia in 1936. (H. Amos)

This view from Custom House Quay at Dover looking across the Granville Dock in the late nineteenth century varies greatly from the scene today. Various craft can be seen including several yachts. The Royal Cinque Ports Yacht Club was founded in 1872 with the Duke of Connaught as Commodore and afterwards gained considerable prestige. Cross-Channel paddle steamers lie beyond in the Wellington Dock. (Dover Standard Series)

Laeisz's nitrate barque *Pisagua* was an unlucky visitor to Dover. Having been
in collision with the P&O SS *Oceana*, which sank off Newhaven on 16 March
1912, she was nursed into Dover by tugs. Her bowsprit, fore royal and topgallant
masts and yards were all carried away in the incident and she also suffered
flooding forward. Her 2,150 tons of cargo were later transferred to the steamer
Magdalena Blumenthal and *Pisagua* was taken into the tidal basin, as shown here,
for repairs. On 3 April 1912 she left under tow for Hamburg.

Right: The *Majestic* was the first steamship to make a Channel crossing in 1815. By 1820 a regular steamer service was in operation. The poster shown dates from the 1830s. Only a few years later the *Magician* was crossing to Boulogne in two hours in good weather. (John Williams collection)

Below: A twin-funnelled paddle steamer lies alongside Custom House Quay in the Granville Dock. Once significant progress had been made on the Admiralty Pier the steamers began to berth there, the first being the *Princess Alice* in 1851.

DOVER HARBOUR.

Given the small size of the ships making the crossing in the nineteenth century, uncomfortable passages were not uncommon, as illustrated here. It was with comfort in mind that three special ships were built in the years 1874–77 supposedly to reduce seasickness. These were the *Castalia*, *Bessemer* and *Calais-Douvres*, but unfortunately none of them were successful.

DOVER. — *Arrival of the Ostend Boat.*

In the Edwardian years, following the arrival of the turbine screw steamers, the paddle steamers were phased out, but some lasted until the start of the First World War. One of the fast Belgian vessels, possibly the *Princesse Henriette*, arrives from Ostende on this occasion while one of the German transatlantic liners lies alongside the Prince of Wales Pier. (Louis Levi)

The first of Denny's steam turbine ferries, *The Queen*, arrived in 1902. She was followed by a whole series, including the *Engadine* and *Invicta*. The *Victoria*, also one of these triple-screw steamers, is here seen occupying the lay-by berth in Wellington Dock. (H. Amos)

Between 1903 and 1906 ships of the Hamburg–American Line, amongst others, called at Dover before sailing to New York. This postcard shows the 16,500-ton SS *Deutschland* berthing alongside the Prince of Wales Pier. The *Amerika* and *Kaiserin Augusta Victoria* also called, the latter, at 24,500 gross tons, the largest ship in the world in 1906. The effect of strong tides whilst manoeuvring in the confines of the new Admiralty Harbour works, however, caused the liners to withdraw, the *Deutschland* having struck one of the piers.

In 1899 work began on the enclosure of 610 acres of water by piers and breakwaters to form the Admiralty Harbour, an enormous undertaking. The contract was awarded to Messrs S. Pearson & Son, whose block-making yard was situated under the east cliff, where land had been reclaimed. (Ramsgate Maritime Museum)

This view of the new east pier head under construction shows the scale of the operation. About 64,000 concrete blocks, weighing in total some 1,920,000 tons, were used to form the bulk of the pier and breakwater walls. (Ramsgate Maritime Museum)

This view of the Admiralty Pier shows the 2,000ft extension in the course of construction. A train is in the pier station and a ship on the berth on the west side of the pier that was used for a time. (Kingsway series)

Exactly the same view after the Marine Station was completed in 1914. For many years all sides of the port were linked by railway, including a track along Marine Parade to the eastern arm. Nowadays no trace of the railway is left. The Marine Station became a cruise ship terminal in 1993. (*Dover Express*)

Above left: Admiral Sir Reginald Bacon was the Senior Naval Officer at Dover for the greater part of the First World War, succeeding Admiral Sir Horace Hood in April 1915. He was the driving force behind the Dover Patrol's anti-submarine activities. He was succeeded by Vice-Admiral Sir Roger Keyes early in 1918.

Above right: Commander Edward R.G. Evans with his destroyer HMS *Broke* and her companion HMS *Swift* were in a major action with German destroyers on the night of 20 April 1917 sinking the *G.42* and *G.85*. During the action the *Broke* rammed the *G.42*. Commanders Evans, above, and Peck were both awarded the DSO for their gallant conduct.

The destroyer HMS *Broke* seen on her trials. A destroyer leader of 1,704 tons, she was building for Chile when the war started and was purchased by the Admiralty. She was re-sold to Chile in 1920, becoming the *Almirante Uribe*.

The Miscellaneous Fleet

At Dover we'd a splendid fleet, but not the orthodox
Regulation fleet of war-time; and some were rather crocks.
When the war broke out the R.N.'s mostly went to Scapa Flow,
And the R.N.R.'s and V.R.'s came to Dover for the show.
>   To swell the Dover Patrol, my lads,
>   To swell the Dover Patrol.
>   But they had jolly good fun when the war had begun,
>   When we served in the Dover Patrol.

We had monitors of M-class and of twelve and fifteen inch,
Which mostly steamed at six knots or seven knots at a pinch.
There were little Coastal Motor-boats and M.L.'s for the screen.
And P-Boats and the Hazard and the C-class submarine,
>   All had a job in the Dover Patrol!
>   A tough time in the Dover Patrol!
>   A time you may bet that was rough, cold, and wet,
>   At sea in the Dover Patrol.

Of Destroyers we'd the Tribals and the ancient Thirty-knotters.
We'd ships that carried kite-balloons and seaplanes for our spotters.
We had steamers armed for boarding to search for contraband,
And armed Drifters and Torpedo boats to lend a helping hand.
>   They all belonged to the Dover Patrol–
>   Did good work in the Dover Patrol.
>   It wasn't all glory, but the commonplace story
>   Of hard work in the Dover Patrol.

The Drifters they caught submarines, and the Paddlers they were willing
To drop their trade of making trippers seasick for a shilling,
To join the Trawlers sweeping mines, and, aided by the yachts,
Their harvest was a good one as the Channel yielded lots.
>   Yes, they came to the Dover Patrol–
>   To the risks of the Dover Patrol.
>   Alas! Many now sleep in the treacherous deep
>   That lies under the Dover Patrol.

The different kinds of ships we had just numbered twenty-four;
And we'd have had some others if there had been any more.
Four hundred ships we totalled in our miscellaneous fleet;
But there's one thing I can tell you – they were precious hard to beat!
>   Beat? Beat the Dover Patrol?
>   Who said beat the Dover Patrol?
>   The Hun couldn't do it–no, not if we knew it,
>   In our day in the Dover Patrol.

Admiral R. Bacon, *The Dover Patrol 1915-1917*

Warships Broken Up by Stanlee at Dover 1918-1926

Name	Vessel type	Tonnage	Date of build	Date sold for breaking up
Belvoir	Minesweeper	750	1917	7.22
C. 9	Submarine	280	1907	7.22
C. 10	Submarine	280	1907	7.22
Canopus	Battleship	12,950	1897	18.2.20
Croome	Minesweeper	750	1917	7.22
Duncan	Battleship	14,000	1901	18.2.20 (arr.18.6.20)
G. 14	Submarine	700	1917	11.3.21
Ghurka (No.7)	Ex-Indian Torpedo boat (1892)	92	1888	27.3.20
Glatton	Coast Defence ship	5,700	1914	Wreck raised and BU 1925-26
Goodwood	Paddle Minesweeper	810	1916	7.22
H. 11	Submarine	364	1915	21
H. 12	Submarine	364	1915	4.22
Haldon	Paddle Minesweeper	810	1916	14.12.21
Hambledon	Minesweeper	750	1917	7.22
Heythrop	Minesweeper	750	1917	7.22
Indomitable	Battle cruiser	17,250	1907	1.12.21 (arr. 30.8.22)
Indus II (ex-*Victorious*)	Repair ship (ex-Battleship)	12,900	1895	4.23
Inflexible	Battle cruiser	17,250	1907	1.12.21
Laertes	Destroyer	982	1913	8.3.22
Lanark	Paddle Minesweeper	820	1917	5.23
Landrail	Destroyer	983	1914	1.12.21
Lingfield	Paddle Minesweeper	810	1916	5.23
Lucifer	Destroyer	987	1913	1.12.21
Morning Star	Destroyer	1,000	1915	1.12.21
Pytchley	Minesweeper	750	1917	7.22
St Vincent	Battleship	19,250	1908	1.12.21
Superb	Battleship	18,600	1907	12.12.22
Swiftsure	Battleship	11,800	1903	18.6.20
T.B. No. 77	Torpedo boat	75	1886	27.3.20
T.B. No. 87	Torpedo boat	85	1889	27.3.20
T.B. No. 109	Torpedo boat	200	1902	27.3.20
T.B. No. 110	Torpedo boat	200	1902	27.3.20
Temeraire	Battleship	18,600	1907	1.12.21
Vengeance	Battleship	12,950	1899	9.1.23

Note: In addition, HMS *Colne*, a destroyer of 560 tons built in 1905, and HMS *Pomone*, a third-class cruiser of 2,135 tons, later reduced to a training hulk, were reported as sold to J.H. Lee of Dover, the former on 4 November 1919 and the latter on 25 October 1922.

Information drawn from *Ships of the Royal Navy*, by J.J. Colledge.

A later steamer built by Denny for the Southern Railway was the *Canterbury* of 1929. She was fitted out to a luxurious standard in order to take the passengers on the cross-Channel leg of the prestigious Golden Arrow-Fliche d'Or rail express between London and Paris which commenced that year. She was broken up in Belgium in 1965. (British Railways)

When the new train ferry dock at Dover began operation in 1936, three specially constructed vessels came into service, the *Hampton Ferry*, *Shepperton Ferry*, shown here, and the *Twickenham Ferry*. As the rail coaches could now be carried aboard, passengers on the 'Night Ferry' could make a relatively undisturbed journey to Dunkirk. This picture was painted by crew-member David Atkinson. (Geoff Michell collection)

The achievement of the evacuation of the British troops from Dunkirk in May 1940 is a significant landmark in British history. Operation Dynamo was superintended by Admiral Ramsay from the castle at Dover and 202,306 in total of British, Commonwealth and allied troops were brought to the port in all manner of craft. This view shows destroyers landing troops; D94 is HMS *Whitehall*.

Troops crowd another ship returning from France but this time there are no steel helmets – only life jackets are worn. Much more optimistic, these men are coming home to Dover for leave in August 1945. (S.A. Lane)

Cross-Channel passenger traffic started to gain momentum again by the late 1940s and more people wanted to take their cars abroad. This Bentley is being loaded aboard the *Autocarrier*. Apart from the train ferries, which could take about twenty-five cars, all vehicles were loaded by crane until the two drive-on berths opened in the Eastern Docks in 1953. (Geoff Michell collection)

The *Lord Warden* was the first drive-on, drive-off car ferry built for the British Transport Commission. Able to carry 120 cars, she started service on the Dover to Boulogne route on 17 June 1952. She was sold to Saudi Arabia in 1980 for further trading. (British Railways)

The Camber area, or Dover's eastern docks, as they became in about 1952 after the two vehicle drive-on, drive-off berths had been completed. The MTB pens are visible at right and a cable ship lies alongside the Post Office quay. The ferry alongside is the *Dinard* of 1924. Converted to a car ferry in 1947, she had hinged stern doors fitted in early 1952 and then ran on the same service as the *Lord Warden* from June 1953.

A part of the eastern docks area photographed in 2008. This picture shows the degree of expansion that has taken place in fifty-six years. The ferries have also increased by some ten times in their tonnage and vehicle capacity. (A.L.)

On the western side of the harbour the Granville Dock was always busy with the import of coal, fresh fruit and vegetables. This picture from the sixties shows three of Fred Olsen's fruit ships and a Stephenson Clarke collier alongside. Nowadays, Olsen's cruise ships call at the port. (Ray Warner)

This recent view of the same part of the harbour shows that the Granville Dock (also the Wellington) and part of the old tidal basin have become a yacht marina. The area to the right of the Prince of Wales Pier was filled in by 1978 to form the Hoverport (now demolished) and the train ferry dock has become an aggregate berth. Further ferry berths are planned for the western docks area, where at the moment only the Admiralty Pier is used by cruise ships. (A.L.)

In consideration of the other companies involved in Channel crossings, two saints from different countries follow. The *St Germain*, shown here, was a train ferry built for the Soc. Nationale de Chemin de Fer Francaise (SNCF) to run in conjunction with the British *Hampton* and *Shepperton Ferries* to Dunkirk. Built in Denmark in 1951 to a modern design she could carry fourteen sleeping cars. She had a long life, not being broken up until 1988. (British Railways)

The Belgian *St Laurent* of 1974 spent a much shorter time on the Channel, being sold to Italy in 1986. Her colours are rather unusual. In 1985 Townsend Thoresen (TT), well known at least for the Townsend part and established at Dover since the 1920s, entered a trading agreement with Regie voor Maritiem Transport (RMT), which entailed their ships having the Belgian funnel and the TT orange hull colour. The agreement lasted for about five years.

The *Côte d'Azur* at almost 9,000 gross tons was for the French SNCF a step up in size in 1981. She became another long-term favourite and was re-named *Seafrance Renoir* when Seafrance emerged out of the terminated Sealink partnership in 1996. She has now been withdrawn from service. (A.L.)

Commandant Michel Vidière keeps watch on the bridge of *Seafrance Renoir* on a regular service to Calais in August 2007. He is now a commandant of the *Seafrance Molière*. (A.L.)

Captain Mike Andrew clears Dover Harbour with *Maersk Delft* outward bound for Dunkirk on a very bright sunny day in September 2007. The amount of bridge equipment is impressive on these modern ferries. Global positioning details, and automatic identification of ships (AIS) and their movements can be combined with the radar display. (A.L.)

Maersk Dover, sister of the *Delft* and *Dunkerque*, lies berthed in her home port. These ships of 35,000 gross tons can carry typically 780 passengers, 200 cars and 120 trucks, but obviously vehicle loadings can vary. Their draught increases by about 1m from the empty to the loaded condition. (A.L.)

The Development of Cross-Channel Ferries from Dover, 1818–2009

Name	Vessel Type	Gross Tonnage	Speed (Knots)	Date Built
Rob Roy/Henri Quatre	Paddle Steamer	90	–	1818
Monarch	Paddle Steamer	100	–	1822
Violet	Paddle Steamer	292	12	1843
Vivid	Paddle Steamer	352	13.5	1849
Foam	Paddle Steamer	496	14	1862
Castalia	Paddle Steamer	1,533	11	1874
Bessemer	Paddle Steamer	1,886	18	1875
Calais-Douvres	Paddle Steamer	1,924	13	1877
Invicta	Paddle Steamer	1,197	18.5	1882
Princesse Henriette	Paddle Steamer	1,100	21	1888
Calais-Douvre	Paddle Steamer	1,212	20	1889
Le Nord	Paddle Steamer	2,004	21.5	1898
Queen	Turbine Steamer	1,650	21.75	1902
Engadine	Turbine Steamer	1,676	24	1911
Canterbury	Turbine Steamer	3,071	22	1929
Autocarrier	Steam Car Ferry	985	15	1931
Shepperton Ferry	Steam Turbine Train Ferry	2,938	16.5	1934
Prins Albert	Motor Vessel	2,938	26	1937
Invicta	Steam Turbine	4,178	22	1940
Lord warden	First Ro-Ro Car Ferry	3,332	20	1952
Free Enterprise	Motor Vessel	2,607	18	1962
Free Enterprise IV	Motor Vessel	5,049	20.5	1969
Swift	SRN-4 Hovercraft MkI/MkII	190	65 (max), 58 (service)	1968
The Princess Anne	SRN-4 Hovercraft MkI/MkIII	190/265	65 (max), 58 (service)	1969
Prins Albert	Motor Vessel	6,019	22	1978
Spirit of Free Enterprise	Motor Vessel	7,951	22	1980
St Christopher	Motor Vessel	6,996	19.5	1981
Princess Clementine	Boeing Jetfoil	289	50 (max), 42 (service)	1981
Pride of Dover	Motor Vessel	26,433	22	1987
Hoverspeed Great Britian	Catamaran (74m)	3,003	42 (max), 35 (service)	1990
Prins Filip	Motor Vessel	28,833	21	1991
Rapide	Catamaran	4,305	47 (max)	1996
Seafrance Rodin	Motor Vessel	33,796	25	2001
Maersk Dunkerque	Motor Vessel	35,923	25	2005
Norman Arrow	Catamaran (112m)	10,000	40	2009

The Royal Navy has not had a base at Dover for many years. A flotilla of BYMS minesweepers was based there towards the end of the war and a salvage depot remained until 1973. Naval vessels still occasionally call, either on courtesy or ceremonial visits. HMS *Illustrious* visited the port in March 2001. (A.L.)

The only MOD-contracted work still carried out at Dover is for fast boats to guard the Hythe and Lydd gunnery ranges and prevent yachtsmen and others from getting too close when firing is taking place. Smit's have the contract to provide the range safety boats *Smit Rother*, *Smit Romney* and *Smit Stour*. Water jet propulsion gives them a top speed of about 40 knots. (A.L.)

The English Channel is the main highway for shipping serving all of northern Europe. As some 500 ships may pass Dover every day, they are regulated in a mandatory separation zone with south-west and north-east lanes. Ferry traffic must very frequently cross these lanes. This picture shows a Hoverspeed Seacat and a P&O ferry crossing the south-west lane about six miles from Dover. (A.L.)

Dover has welcomed cruise ships for many years and now has two dedicated terminals on the Admiralty Pier. Visiting companies include Costa Cruises (now part of the Carnival Group), Norwegian Cruise Line, Fred Olsen and Saga Shipping of Folkestone. The latter's *Saga Ruby*, built originally as the *Vistafjord* in 1973, has very elegant lines. (A.L.)

P&O Cruises' *Royal Princess* of 44,000 tons built in 1982 was used as a model for the berthing requirements and design of the first cruise terminal at Dover in 1993. (A.L.)

Cruise ships have increased significantly in size over the past sixteen years. One of these larger vessels is the MSC *Poesia* which arrived for naming by Sophia Loren on 4 April 2008. She was launched at St Nazaire on 30 August 2007, having a length of 294m and a gross tonnage of 92,400. *Carnival Splendor* is the largest cruise liner to call so far at Dover, having a gross tonnage of 112,000. (A.L.)

A recent ship to join the French cross-Channel ferry fleets is the *Seafrance Molière* which commenced sailings in the late summer of 2008. A very attractive-looking vessel, she was built in 2002 as the *Superfast X*. The cruise ship in the background is the *Costa Marina*. (A.L.)

No fast craft crossed the Channel after the departure of *Speed 1* in November 2008 until 6 June 2009 when LD ferries introduced the largest vessel so far built by Incat in Tasmania. The 112m *Norman Arrow* is run by a British subsidiary of the French operator and can carry trucks as well as cars, the first catamaran on the route to do so. *Norman Arrow* has an operational speed of about 40 knots. This vessel was, however, transferred to the Portsmouth–Le Havre service in November 2009. (A.L.)

Left: The port control staff are responsible for safe navigation within the harbour and also the approaches. Equipped with the latest electronic aids for their vessel traffic management system, the tower at the end of the eastern arm also enjoys an exceptional view of the harbour. On watch are Richard McGannan, seated, and standing, from left, Simon Phillips, Mike Pascall and David Standen. (A.L.)

Below: The Port of Dover has the usual mandatory pilotage requirements for vessels whose masters do not regularly visit the port. Their new launch *Dovorian* acts both as pilot launch and harbour service craft. Her mate, Dominic Kent, has just seen the pilot safely aboard the fruit ship *Hornbay*. (A.L.)

8

FOLKESTONE

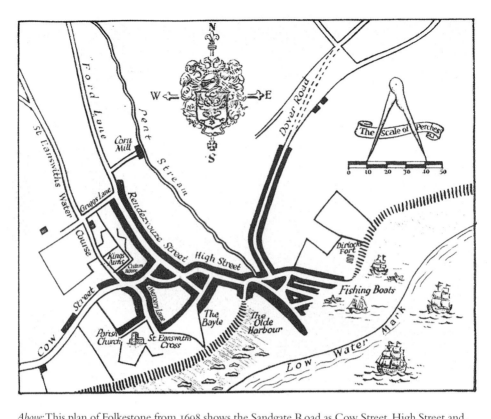

Above: This plan of Folkestone from 1698 shows the Sandgate Road as Cow Street. High Street and Mercery Lane (now Church Street) are recognisable as is the general line of the Dover Road. The Pent stream suggests a means of flushing silt from the harbour as in other ports. At this time the town was at a very early stage of development.

Below: An etching from 1831 made of Folkestone Harbour at low water before the arrival of the railway. The houses of the fishermen in the Stade are represented in detail and some features are recognisable today. When the South Eastern Railway bought the harbour in 1843 it was in an advanced state of decay. (E. W. Cooke)

An early cross-Channel steamer berthed in front of the Custom House. Following the arrival of the railway at the quayside in 1849 via a new, large swing bridge, a new Custom House and railway station were built on the south quay by 1854. After this date the South Eastern Railway developed the harbour considerably, building a pier extending seawards as at Dover in 1863. This was further increased in length in 1905.

A mixed group of passengers awaits the berthing of the cross-Channel boat in 1886. (*Illustrated London News*)

40 FOLKESTONE. — *Arrival of Turbine Steamer.* — LL.

About twenty years later than the previous illustration, one of the Denny-built turbine steamers, probably the *Onward*, lies alongside the pier. In 1918 this vessel caught fire and capsized here, presenting salvors with a major problem. (Louis Levi)

This illustration of the drawing room car of a Folkestone Express suggests considerable opulence. It appears Edwardian, thus showing that Pullman trains to the coast pre-dated the 'Golden Arrow' by many years. (McCorquodale & Co.)

FOLKESTONE CROSS CHANNEL STEAMER, ISLE OF THANET, LEAVING QUAY.

The Southern Railway steamer *Isle of Thanet* leaving the harbour. Built by Denny's of Dumbarton in 1925, she worked mainly from Folkestone and served as a hospital ship during the war. A 22-knot vessel of 2,789 gross tons, her final years were spent running to both Calais and Boulogne. She was eventually sold for scrap in 1964. (British Railways)

Her French companion for a time was the *Cote d'Azur* of 4,037 tons, built in 1951. Between October 1952 and May 1960 this vessel carried the outward 'Golden Arrow' passengers from Folkestone to Calais. She was replaced in 1972 by the car ferry *Chartres*. The 'Golden Arrow' ran for the last time on 30 September of that year. (British Railways)

FISHING QUARTER, FOLKESTONE HARBOUR 49

As in many of the other ports, fishing has been a long-established occupation at Folkestone. The fishing fleet is here gathered in the inner harbour in the 1930s. At that time there were about forty luggers, nearly all motorised. Amongst this group are: *Happy Return* (FE5), *G.C.P.* (FE38), *Jessica* (FE42), *Florence Rosalind* (FE55), *Carn Du* (FE 67), *Three Brothers* (FE 93) and *Dayspring* (FE217). *Happy Return* and *Three Brothers* are still in existence. (Norman Series)

Although the number of vessels has declined, trawlers still work from Folkestone, the only seafaring activity that remains. The *Viking Princess*, *Rowena* and *Lady Patricia* (HL 16) are three of the eight that fish today mainly for cod, sole and skate. (A.L.)